"This is a truly revolutionary step through the process of crochet business. Elisa has c1 necessary information that is success. This is the book I wi ing out!"

CW00540112

— Holly Faith Lanier, owner of Storyland Amis

"A strategy blueprint every crocheter needs to know. This positive-thinking book transforms your mindset from a no-go to a LET'S GO! attitude. It's the best book out there that teaches you how to market your crochet pattern business."

— Irina from @BlueRabbitToys

"My first thought when I saw this book was, "Where was this book when I decided to start my crochet pattern business?" The book really does cover everything to start a crochet pattern business, from how to start designing, to writing your patterns, to photography and marketing. There are also images and diagrams, which are great visual aids that add an extra level of clarity. This is a perfect guide for new and existing crochet business owners, like myself, to learn more about the processes to achieve our dreams and goals of running a successful crochet pattern business."

— Chloe from @EmiCreationsByChloe

"A great guide for starting up your crochet business. This book will help you determine your next steps for success!"

— Amy from @curiouspapaya

"If you want to learn how to start a crochet pattern business, this amazing book will help you how to get started. Making money while doing what you love is not a dream, you can make it a reality! There is a lot of helpful step-by-step information to figure out how to get started and how to grow your business successfully. Make your dream come true!"

– JuliaKa from @JuliaKaPattern

CROCHET YOUR WAY TO A BUYER'S HEART WITH AMIGURUMI

8 Revolutionary Steps to Jump Start Your
Crochet Business:
How to Design and Make Money Selling
Crochet Patterns

BY ELISA ROSE

"I have no special
talent. I am
passionately curious."
Albert Einstein

Contents

INTRODUCTION:
Hello, Crochet World

You love to crochet. You may be a crochet addict and not even know it. Your family doesn't understand your obsession with crocheting, but other crocheters get it. You'd rather spend hours walking through the yarn aisle at Hobby Lobby, Michaels, or Jo-Ann Fabrics than shopping for clothes and shoes at the mall. Instead of aimlessly browsing the internet and buying random stuff on Amazon like everyone else, you're on Ravelry and Etsy scouring for crochet patterns. You have enough crochet patterns to keep you busy for over two lifetimes. You probably have a ton of yarn stashed away, hidden from your significant other throughout the house — more yarn than you can count and enough to circle Earth five times. Now you're thinking about taking your talents to a whole new level, crochet designing.

You're excited to start designing crochet patterns — and you could make some extra cash while you're at it. You say to yourself, "I think I can do this!" Pat yourself on the back. Applause! You picture a parade marching down Bourbon Street, hearing the sounds of trumpets and people throwing confetti and beads, celebrating with you like it's Mardi Gras.

Then, you take a step back and ask yourself, "Can I do this? The crochet market is too saturated. There are too many crochet designers out there. There's just no way I can compete with them." Your marching band and Mardi Gras entourage start to retreat and disappear into the distance. Second-guessing yourself will only hold you back from starting your crochet design business, so find your confidence again and pull yourself together. The first step to any adventure is to start.

Think back to when you first picked up that crochet hook. It's frustrating learning how to crochet for the first time — whether you watched YouTube videos or learned from your grandmother. There were times you wondered why you even picked up this hobby in the first place. All crocheters go through the same thing — figuring out how to find that comfort level of holding a crochet hook in one hand and overcoming that awkward feeling of securing the hold of yarn in the other.

Crochet designing is no different.

Anyone and everyone experiences the same self-doubt and the fear of not succeeding. It is human nature to have these feelings, especially when you don't feel like an expert in this industry. It's why this book is so crucial to have!

The best tips and tricks for becoming a good pattern writer and successful online seller are shared here. This book walks you through 8 essential steps to succeed in designing, writing, and selling crochet patterns using the Sprinkle approach. That's right, S.P.R.I.N.K.L.E.

S….. is for Shapes and Stitches

P….. is for Pop

R….. is for Report Format

I….. is for Inviting

N….. is for Niche

K….. is for Kinks and Kick-off

L….. is for Launch

E….. is for Empowerment, Embrace, and Engage

The tools in the Sprinkle approach will help you attract potential pattern buyers, make them fall in love with your designs, and have your contributions impact the crochet world. What are you waiting for? A sprinkle of success waits for no crocheter! If you're ready and pumped to take on the crochet design world, then let's get started!

"Once we accept our limits, we go beyond them." Albert Einstein

---

CHAPTER 1

TURN YOUR PASSION INTO PROFIT

"Never give up on a dream just because of the time it will take to accomplish it. The time will pass anyway." Earl Nightingale

1. POWER OF PASSIVE INCOME

Crocheting can be quite an obsession. Instead of counting sheep at night, you're thinking about your next crochet project or how many handmade items you need to make for your kid's classroom party. You're confident in your crochet skills, and you may have even sold a few items to family and friends, at craft fairs, or on Etsy. Now, you're curious about dabbling in a new avenue of the crochet business — designing. Other crocheters are doing it. So why not give it a go yourself? Why are crocheters exploring this path of designing and selling patterns? What's so appealing about selling patterns rather than selling finished items?

First, think of the disadvantages of selling handmade items. A few things that come to mind are the cost of yarn, the time it takes to complete hand making an item, and the commitment to finishing the article on time. It's the dreaded trifecta: time, cost, and labor. In the end, it just might not be worth it to drive to the craft store, buy yarn, and spend hours making something when you don't have a guarantee of making much of a profit.

If you consider how much you are likely to get paid per hour of crochet work, plus the cost of materials, there's not much money to be made. Assuming it takes 6 hours to crochet a doll and you set your hourly wage at $7.25, the federal minimum wage in the US, you'd need to charge at least around $45 for making the doll, not including materials and overhead costs. How many customers are willing to pay $45, $65, or $100 for a handmade doll?

Selling physical items can also be stressful. You're on the clock to deliver your products on time. There's always the time constraint and pressure of providing a quality output by a specified date, whether for a craft fair event you signed up for or an item someone paid you to make. Because there is a deadline involved, there's doubt about whether you gave yourself enough lead time. There are also a lot of logistics involved when selling finished items at a physical or online marketplace. You have to set up your booth or "storefront" at every craft fair, and there are safety consumer product rules and shipping that must be managed for an online store.

Also, consider putting yourself in the consumers' shoes. But more specifically, what are the reasons why customers buy your handmade items? A lot of craft fairs you participate in as a booth seller are usually run by local organizations or charities. People attend these events to support their local community. They're not looking to spend a lot of money, and to be honest, they're not here for you. They go to these events to have a good time and buy a few things to support their community. People usually buy things from you because they're already at the event and something you have out caught their eye. You're lucky when you get those impulse buyers who don't care how much the item costs. And it's unlikely that you'll get people to buy your high-end items at these low-key events.

Another downside to making and selling finished items is making the same item over and over. Some people don't mind making fifty of the same thing, like winter hats, coffee cozy sleeves, or amigurumi holiday pumpkins, whales, and turtles, especially if they can do it in under an hour. Some, however, need to keep it interesting and varied. Making the same item again can be tedious. It's no longer challenging; some people have a short attention span, or making one item is enough and they are just ready to move on to the next project. Crocheting the same thing over and over can, at times, become a chore and wear some people down. The fun and excitement of crocheting can eventually be lost to the routine of "mass production." The novelty of making something new is now lost. The point of a hobby is to enjoy it and not feel like you're a human factory, continuously grinding out the same thing to make a buck.

Lastly, the sad reality is that there's the possibility of buyers bargaining for a lower price and not valuing handmade craftsmanship. Crocheters who make and sell finished items tell themselves they're in it for the passion, not the profit. Many people sell handmade stuff because it's gratifying and validating when people like your work. Crocheters often try to convince themselves that money isn't the primary motivator for taking up the hobby because it's enjoyable.

"The best way to create the future is to create it." Peter Drucker

---

Advantages of Crochet Designing

So what's so great about crochet designing? Think about working on a new pattern for the first time. Following and crocheting from a new pattern is always exciting (and maybe a little daunting). You've never crocheted this item before, and even though you have a reference image for how it's supposed to look, you're anxious to see how yours turns out. Designing and creating your own pattern is like crocheting a new pattern every time. It's like picking up a book you've never read or putting pieces of a puzzle together for the first time.

You never know how things will turn out until you're done. Some crocheters like to challenge themselves by trying new things. They like the unknown. These are some reasons why designing and pattern writing piques people's interest when venturing into a crochet business.

Now consider the consumer's perspective, more specifically, the *crocheter* as a consumer. Think about your folder, binder, and tablet device — your library of crochet patterns. How many patterns do you own? And how many patterns have you collected from the same crochet designer? The answer is probably: too many to count and a *lot*. Price is also often overlooked. Crochet consumers are like Starbucks drinkers. Many crocheters don't mind paying an average of $5-$6 per pattern, just like a Starbucks drinker who doesn't mind shelling out that amount for a grande mocha latte. These are the customers you want to focus on; this is the market you want to be in. Focus more on the repeat shoppers rather than the occasional shoppers.

Lastly, one of the biggest motivators for designing and selling patterns is the ability to make money passively. Selling a physical object is a one-time sale only. You can hand make and sell another of the same item, but once you give away the physical object, the sale is complete and you have to buy more materials and reinvest your time to make another item. On the other hand, a single pattern can sell over and over again with virtually no additional effort after the initial work is done. Imagine. One good pattern can generate money on its own, more than a gorgeous blanket worth hundreds!

"Don't judge each day by the harvest you reap but the seeds you plant." Robert Louis Stevenson

Passive vs. Active Income

So what is passive income? Before getting into what passive income is, it's easier to understand and relate to active income. Active income is when money is earned based on a task or service you provide in a specific time frame. In the real world, this is your daily 9-to-5 job. You most likely work for someone and get paid a salary or hourly wage for your time. Active income is typically steady and predictable. You know when and how much money is coming in.

The act of making finished crochet items is somewhat considered an active income, depending on how steady your item orders are. Whether in person or online, you are selling physical items at a marketplace. There is a transactional exchange of hands between you and the customer — your crochet work for their cash. The task rendered, or your 9-to-5 in this case, is completing the physical item you made, and someone then pays you for that item.

One of the most significant drawbacks to active income is that you can't physically work forever. And, because crocheting involves working with your hands, making and selling crocheted items is a less favorable option for a crochet business in the long run. This is especially true if you experience arthritis, carpal tunnel, tendonitis, or any other debilitating injury or illness.

Passive income is an opportunity for crocheters to consider. Not only do you still get to share your craft with others, but you're also able to share your knowledge with others. Passive income is when you've completed a service or task in the past and continue to make money with minimal effort to maintain it. For example, you design one pattern and then move on to the next pattern, and the next, while still making money on your first pattern. You're automatically generating money for something you previously worked on a month ago, two years ago, or even seven years ago.

"The two most powerful warriors are patience and time."
Leo Tolstoy, War and Peace

2. PATIENCE IS A VIRTUE

The 80-20 Rule

People get discouraged from pursuing a passive income path because the money that can be made isn't immediately tangible. The temptation of instant gratification is too hard to avoid. Another downside is that you don't know how much you'll earn, and you might not see any financial return for a while.

It's only natural to focus on making money right away. But good things come to those who wait. How long is that wait time, though? Some people are turned away from crochet designing because they don't see the benefits right away. Yes, there's some work at the beginning, but the money will come.

Putting in the initial work and seeing financial results through passive income is like any other life lesson journey. It's important to distinguish the difference and expectations between financial results and financial success. Your crochet design efforts will produce financial results. There's no doubt you will have people buying your patterns. As for financial success, the measure of success is relative. Does financial success mean quitting your day job, being able to afford a nice vacation, or just a nice-to-have fund to offset your yarn purchases?

It's ironic that making money isn't the top priority when it comes to selling physical items, but when it comes to designing, making money feels like it's the main goal. Results will come first. Success, however you define it, comes later. You'll achieve financial success by working hard, learning from your failures, and not giving up.

A meaningful life lesson is to assess the 80-20 rule, particularly when pursuing a crochet business. The Pareto Principle (the official name of the 80-20 rule) is about identifying your strengths and weaknesses and ensuring you maximize value as efficiently as possible. It's about how much effort you put in to get the best results and how much input is exerted to get the optimal output. 80% of outcomes come from 20% of causes. That means about 80% of your success will come from a relatively small number of factors.

The key to applying the Pareto Principle to your business, and therefore to achieving success, is to identify those factors that impact your business most, and then adjust your strategies accordingly. Your goal is not to expend effort that goes to waste. Be an active observer. It's important to identify the areas that warrant an investment of time/effort to get the results you want.

Maybe you're a great crochet designer, and maybe you can write the perfect crochet pattern. But if you don't have an audience to read your pattern, it doesn't matter how great of a designer and writer you are. Many factors impact people wanting to see and purchase your pattern. Before anyone gets to see how great a designer and pattern writer you are, you have to bring traffic to your pattern. Consumers always judge a book by its cover. It's all about getting yourself noticed. Good marketing is key to driving traffic to your selling platform — it's not just about the quality of your content or your technical ability.

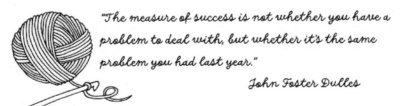

"The measure of success is not whether you have a problem to deal with, but whether it's the same problem you had last year."

John Foster Dulles

The concept behind the 80-20 rule is to avoid spreading yourself too thin and instead focus on the few areas that will help get the attention you deserve and to bring in traffic. Pinpointing where to improve and successfully achieving those milestones to help bring in those customers doesn't mean the same efforts will always be your magic weapon. Applying the 80-20 rule boils down to your persistence and consistency. Constantly reassess and evaluate those checked-off boxes to ensure you meet your goals.

"The successful man will profit from his mistakes and try again in a different way." Dale Carnegie

Kill Two Birds with One Stone

Passive income is an income stream that all crocheters should consider. It's a missed opportunity for crocheters not to seek out. Comparing time, effort, and cost, crochet designing makes more money than selling physical items. If you are creating custom orders based on your own designs for clients, you might as well take the time to write down the pattern you are making.

Crochet designing is a valuable business opportunity for crocheters. One revenue stream can actually allow you to conduct and build multiple revenue streams. Once you start making money from crochet designing, other opportunities will present themselves.

Designing and pattern writing is such a lucrative business because it leverages two favorable factors. First, designing a crochet pattern can easily be reproduced, replicated, and repeated. (Yes, really!) Second, technology-based information sharing allows the reproduction, replication, and repetition of patterns to be distributed to the masses with minimal effort. It's not like you have to handwrite or print every pattern and physically mail it to customers!

Imagine how many ways one pattern can be viewed and disseminated. You have hard copy books, online magazines and ebooks, electronic files, vlogs and blogs, physical and online marketplace platforms, emails, and social media outlets such as YouTube, TikTok, Pinterest, and Instagram. With the click of one button, how many people can be reached simultaneously and instantaneously? This is the power of combining pattern selling and passive income!

You may initially start selling patterns on one online marketplace, but why sell on one when you can easily sell the same patterns on two or more platforms? It's like being in two places at once. Many designers may be satisfied with just two platforms and stop there with their business endeavors, even though they can tap into so many other avenues. Some designers go even further and sell e-books and print copies of their patterns through Amazon. If print copies are something you wish to pursue, knocking on craft store doors is another consideration for an income stream. Big box stores may be more challenging to engage with, but there are hundreds of mom-and-pop yarn stores to consider. Besides self-publishing, you could also consider a revenue path of publishing patterns in magazines and receiving royalty fees.

Through these various channels, you can then direct customers to your social media accounts and your website, blog, or You-Tube videos. And, of course, through these social media platforms, there is the eventual opportunity to monetize through Google ads, affiliations, and sponsorships.

By exploring a business in designing and selling patterns, you'll unexpectedly see surprising results you didn't know you had in you! Success will truly follow. Generating revenue through passive income will continue to grow in multiples with the designing and pattern-writing business. Picture the positive ripple effects crochet design can offer you. These are your creations and patterns; why not diversify and sell your talents through multiple platforms and income streams? Take advantage of what you can do with all these opportunities.

ACTIVE INCOME	**PASSIVE INCOME**
☑ Paid for work actively performed	☑ Paid for work already performed
☑ Expected, consistent, and linear income growth	☑ Inconsistent but unlimited income growth
☑ Low upfront effort	☑ Higher upfront effort
☑ Required to work to make money	☑ Doing something else while making money

CHAPTER 2

S IS FOR SHAPES AND STITCHES

"Energy and persistence conquer all things." Benjamin Franklin

---

1. THE STUDENT BECOMES THE MASTER

Walk Before You Run

Before starting this crochet design business, the obvious must be stated. Hone in on the craft of crochet before picking up that pen and paper to start sketching and writing. Though you may be a beginner in designing and writing crochet patterns, you should at least consider yourself a beginner-intermediate or intermediate level crocheter. The more practice you have and the greater variety of crochet projects you do, the more knowledge you can apply to your designs. It's crucial to actually know the craft before anything else.

Practice Makes Perfect

It is beneficial to practice crocheting the same items of existing patterns at least two times. For example, if you enjoy making baby lovey blankets, crochet the same one again. Though it may sound a little contradictory from Chapter 1, as you might get bored making the same bumble bee or Pokemon ball over and over, this repetition helps refine your craftsmanship; but more importantly, it gives you a deeper understanding of reading patterns.

So why make the same, repeated crochet doll more than once? Why not crochet many other patterns instead? According to the Oxford dictionary, the definition of crochet is: "a handicraft in which yarn is made up into a patterned fabric by looping yarn with a hooked needle." The primary keyword here is *handicraft*, or a "craft by hand." Because crochet involves repetitive hand movements, muscle memory kicks in, and your motor skills start to remember the same actions. And as you repeatedly perform the same motions, your quality of work for that same design improves over time. For example, if you made four of the same bumble bees, your gaps or holes are tighter and smaller. Your tension becomes more consistent, and the stuffing inside the toy becomes less visible. You naturally become more familiar with that particular design and shape for that specific amigurumi bee when you follow the same steps. Take a photo and compare the first bee you ever made with your most recent one. Hands down, you'll notice drastic improvements.

Besides improving your craftsmanship, crocheting the same pattern also gives you a better perspective of interpreting the pattern. It allows you to understand how the object is structured or shaped. When you work on a new pattern, you "blindly" follow the instructions step by step, not knowing nor really caring what the pattern means. All you initially care about is making sure your amigurumi looks like the one in the photo. As you continue with the pattern, sometimes you may be faced with a situation where you ask yourself if you're following the steps correctly. Maybe your work in progress looks a bit strange to you at the moment; you can't fully picture how your work will turn out like the one in the photo, but you continue to follow the pattern anyway. As you're close to finishing, you're more confident with the outcome and you feel a sense of relief knowing you followed the instructions correctly. When you follow the same pattern the second time around, you have a *much* clearer picture and understanding of why the pattern was written this and that way. You know where in the pattern things begin to take shape. The pattern now makes more sense to you. It's similar to when people read the same book twice; reading a book over again helps improve overall comprehension. The reader not only has a new insight into the book, but the reader also appreciates how the book is written, what the meaning behind a particular passage is trying to say, and where specific scenes intensify the story plot.

"The only source of knowledge is experience." Albert Einstein

---

Know What You Eat

Another critical factor to consider when improving your craft is understanding the mechanics of different stitches. The stitches you choose can really change up the look of your designs, but there's also a method to the madness. For example, you should know how to do basic stitches like single (US) and double crochet; but it's also helpful to understand the height progression of stitches like the slip stitch, half double crochet, and double crochet. A deeper understanding of stitch construction helps with designing slants and angular elements when crocheting in the same row.

Knowing the height progression is helpful for making scarves and hair bangs for dolls. But did you know the quickest crochet stitch is the triple/treble (US) crochet? Crocheting this way not only saves you time, but also yarn, compared to working in repeated single crochets. But depending on what you're making, the triple crochet can affect the structural build of your work. For example, it might work better for scarves and handbags than for amigurumi, where gaps and holes would be too noticeable.

It's worth thinking about how stitches will affect your design work. Just like people on diets, people become more aware of what they eat. The more you know about making the stitches, the more insight and flexibility you have when creating your designs and how you approach them.

When in Rome

Once you're really comfortable crocheting, the most crucial skill for designing is knowing how to read and understand patterns, as this is the foundation of writing patterns. Crocheting freehand and coming up with new designs might come naturally to some people, but being able to write down your design and have others replicate it is a whole different skill.

It is essential to know the crochet language and its terminology and abbreviations. For example, did you know that the US crochet terminology differs from the UK? If you've never heard of this, continue brushing up on your crochet knowledge. You don't have to know both crochet terms. Still, knowing which language you're writing in is important, as it impacts how your designs look and which audience you're targeting. For example, a single crochet (sc) in American terminology is a double crochet (dc) in British terminology.

Common Amigurumi Crochet Stitches Crosswalk Map

Symbol	US Abbr.	US	UK	Turning ch and working first st on foundation
⬯	ch	chain		-
●	sl st	slip st	slip stitch (sl st, ss)	-
X, +	sc	single crochet	double crochet (dc)	1 ch, 2nd ch from hook
T	hdc	half double crochet	half treble (htr)	2 ch, 3rd ch from hook
⅄	dc	double crochet	treble (tr)	3 ch, 4 ch from hook
⅄	tr	treble crochet	double treble (dtr)	4 ch, 5th ch from hook

Just like learning a language, you may be able to speak fluently, but that doesn't necessarily mean you know how to read or write well. For crochet, even if you have the talent and skill set to design, it's important to learn to read a pattern; otherwise, how are you going to write it out for others to understand?

It is also important to become fluent in the everyday speech of crochet, the jargon of crochet and yarn enthusiasts. Knowing catchphrases and slang that your customers and all crafters know ensures you can communicate successfully. For example, you need to know WIP (work in progress) and frogging. Never heard of frogging? Frogging is where you unravel the yarn, or rip apart the project you are working on. Hence, ripping out your work is the onomatopoeia, or the sound of what a frog makes — rip-it, rip-it…*ribbit, ribbit.* When you are well-versed and your knowledge comes across naturally with your speech/writing, you establish immediate credibility. In addition, when you present yourself as someone immersed in the language of crochet, your passion for the craft will be evident and other crocheters will more likely be interested in your patterns.

SLANG	MEANING
AMI	Short for amigurumi.
CAL	Crochet-along (or follow along).
Crojo	Crochet mojo. Your drive and motivation to crochet.
FO	Finished object.
Frog	Rip out your work. The sound of what a frog makes "rip it".
HOTH/ FOTH	Hot (or fresh) off the hook.
TOAD	Trash object abandoned in disgust. A failed project.
UFO	Unfinished object. An incomplete project.
WIP	Work in progress.
Yarn barf (or vomit)	A bunched-up mess of yarn pulled from the center of the yarn ball.
Yarn chicken	Finishing a row, hoping the yarn doesn't run out.

Having a solid foundation of the basics of crochet, from physical crochet skills to reading patterns, is fundamental to your success as a designer and a pattern writer. The more you learn, the more you earn. The more you know, the better your designs will look and the higher quality your patterns will be. Establish the groundwork first before getting started. This new adventure may be exciting yet daunting, but this is a WIP! Yes, mistakes will be made along the way, but you pick yourself up and learn from them. Enjoy this new venture and have fun with it!

2. THE ART OF CROCHET IS IN THE MATH

Crochet is an art form. But if you think about it, crochet is a science — well, math — and not just an art form. Crochet is a craft consisting of repeated patterns from yarn. These patterns are repeated decorative designs. Math is the knowledge that includes numbers, formulas, shapes, and spaces. Crochet has numbers and counting. *Check!* Crochet has shapes and spaces.

Check! And lastly, crochet has formulas. *Check!* Therefore, crochet must be a math art!

Know Your Shapes

It is essential to familiarize yourself with basic crochet shapes. The most common shape pattern in amigurumi is the sphere. Other key shapes are the cone, cylinder, and oval. To understand basic shapes is to understand the method or math concepts behind them. The fundamental principle to forming shape and volume in crochet pieces is to know how to increase and decrease. Therefore, the key to designing and writing crochet patterns is understanding how to increase and decrease stitch counts to create shapes.

SHAPE	COMMON USE
Sphere	Ball, body and head of doll
Cylinder	Body limbs (i.e., arms and legs), rounded ears
Cone	Witch hat, spikes, horns

An increase is when two (or more) stitches are worked into one stitch. Adding a stitch increases the length of a row or expands the volume in a round. A decrease is when two (or more) stitches from a prior row/round are crocheted together into one stitch. Removing a stitch shortens the length of a row or narrows the volume in a round.

STITCH	ABBREVIATION	MEANING
increase	inc	Adds a stitch (typically two or more) into a row for length or round for expansion
decrease	dec	Removes a stitch (typically two or more) from the row to shorten the length or to close in (narrow) on the volume

Behind the Magic 6 Ball

Amigurumi balls are made by increasing or decreasing the number of stitches in each row to create the ball's shape and form, and the height is determined by the total number of rounds. When reading an amigurumi ball pattern closely, the pattern is dissected into three sections: (1) 6 rounds to create the expansion of the circle, (2) 6 rounds to create the height of the ball, and (3) 6 rounds to close in on the ball.

A basic ball pattern typically looks like this:

Round 1	6 sc in the mr. (6 sts)
Round 2	[inc] repeat 6 times. (12 sts)
Round 3	[1 sc, inc] repeat 6 times. (18 sts)
Round 4	[2 sc, inc] repeat 6 times. (24 sts)
Round 5	[3 sc, inc] repeat 6 times. (30 sts)
Round 6	[4 sc, inc] repeat 6 times. (36 sts)
Round 7	36 sc
Round 8	36 sc
Round 9	36 sc
Round 10	36 sc
Round 11	36 sc
Round 12	36 sc
Round 13	36 sc
Round 14	[4 sc, dec] repeat 6 times. (30 sts)
Round 15	[3 sc, dec] repeat 6 times. (24 sts)
Round 16	[2 sc, dec] repeat 6 times. (18 sts)
Round 17	[1 sc, dec] repeat 6 times. (12 sts)
Round 18	[dec] repeat 6 times. (6 sts).

Diagram of a Symmetrical Sphere

③ Rounds 13–18 (or 6 rows)

The ball closes in

② Rounds 7–12 (or 6 rows)

① Rounds 1–6 (or 6 rows)

The ball expands out

1. Round 1 through Round 6 (a total of 6 rows) widens and creates the lower half of the ball. The first six rounds create a 2-dimensional effect, or flatness of a circle. As the number of stitches increases by 6, the wider the two-dimensional circle gets.

2. Round 7 through Round 12 (a total of 6 rows) repeat the same number of stitches and the same number of rows to create the proportional height of the ball, as the 3-dimensional effect begins to take form.

3. Round 13 through Round 18 (a total of 6 rows) is like a mirror image, or flipped, of Round 1 through Round 6. This section closes in and creates the upper half of the ball.

Math for Basic Increases

Let's conceptualize how to create the expansion of the ball. First, remember how the pattern for the first 6 rows (Round 1 through Round 6) was written:

Round 1   6 sc in the mr. (6 sts)

Round 2   [inc] repeat 6 times. (12 sts)

Round 3   [1 sc, inc] repeat 6 times. (18 sts)

Round 4	[2 sc, inc] repeat 6 times. (24 sts)
Round 5	[3 sc, inc] repeat 6 times. (30 sts)
Round 6	[4 sc, inc] repeat 6 times. (36 sts)

Round 1 starts with just creating our base on a magic loop. (There is nothing to increase in Round 1.) An increase in a round is initiated in Round 2. From here on, we then set an increment counter of 1 in every round.

The pattern calls for adding a stitch (or +1 sc) for every repeat (or 6 times) to the round. The repeated pattern shows a total of 6 counts in each round, therefore, expanding the ball by 6 stitches per round.

The detailed math steps are described below:

Round	Pattern	(+) Counter #	Math Translation
Round 1	6 sc in mr.		6 sts
Round 2	[inc] repeat 6 times.	(0)	[(0 sts) + 2 sts] x6 = 12 sts
Round 3	[1 sc, inc] repeat 6 times.	(I)	[(1 st) + 2 sts] x6 = 18 sts
Round 4	[2 sc, inc] repeat 6 times.	(II)	[(2 sts) + 2 sts] x6 = 24 sts
Round 5	[3 sc, inc] repeat 6 times.	(III)	[(3 sts) + 2 sts] x6 = 30 sts
Round 6	[4 sc, inc] repeat 6 times.	(IIII)	[(4 sts) + 2 sts] x6 = 36 sts

* where inc = 2 sts

Math for Basic Decreases

The decrease pattern is just like the increase pattern, except it removes a total of 6 stitches from each round instead of adding them. Remember that the last 6 rows (Round 13 through Round 18) is a flipped image of the first 6 rows (Round 1 through Round 6), eventually working back down to the original count of 6 sts.

Rnd 1	6 sc in the mr. (6 sts)	Rnd 13	36 sc
Rnd 2	[inc] repeat 6 times. (12 sts)	Rnd 14	[4 sc, dec] repeat 6 times. (30 sts)
Rnd 3	[1 sc, inc] repeat 6 times. (18 sts)	Rnd 15	[3 sc, dec] repeat 6 times. (24 sts)
Rnd 4	[2 sc, inc] repeat 6 times. (24 sts)	Rnd 16	[2 sc, dec] repeat 6 times. (18 sts)
Rnd 5	[3 sc, inc] repeat 6 times. (30 sts)	Rnd 17	[1 sc, dec] repeat 6 times. (12 sts)
Rnd 6	[4 sc, inc] repeat 6 times. (36 sts)	**Rnd 18**	**[dec] repeat 6 times. (6 sts)**

Round 13 is the last row with the same number of stitches (36 sts) as the previous round (Round 12). In Round 14, the ball begins to close in. We then apply the same counter number (4) from where we left off (in Round 6). Since we're counting down, a decrement counter of 1 is applied for each new round until the counter is back to zero.

The decreased stitch (or -1 sc) for every repeat (or 6 times) is removed from the round, making the ball shrink by 6 counts. The pattern calls for taking away 6 stitches in each round until the ball is finally closed.

The math steps for decreasing are described below:

Round	Pattern	(-) Counter #	Math Translation
Round 13	36 sc.		36 sts
Round 14	[4 sc, dec] repeat 6 times.	(IIII)	[4 sts + (2 sts - 1 st)] x6 = 30 sts
Round 15	[3 sc, dec] repeat 6 times.	(III)	[3 sts + (2 sts - 1 st)] x6 = 24 sts
Round 16	[2 sc, dec] repeat 6 times.	(II)	[2 sts + (2 sts - 1 st)] x6 = 18 sts
Round 17	[1 sc, dec] repeat 6 times.	(I)	[1 st + (2 sts - 1 st)] x6 = 12 sts
Round 18	[dec] repeat 6 times.	(0)	[0 st + (2 sts - 1 st)] x6 = 6 sts,

* where dec = (2 sts - 1 st)

Pattern for the Evenly Divided:
Multiples and Factors

Trace back to your elementary school years. Think way back to when you were learning about the principles of multiplication and division, and remember the mnemonic device for the order of operations: Please Excuse My Dear Aunt Sally (or parenthesis, exponents, multiplication, division, addition, subtraction). Crochet applies similar concepts when writing crochet patterns.

The most common math concepts used in crochet patterns are multiples and factors. A multiple is a number that you get when you multiply a certain number by another number, e.g. multiples of 5 are: 5 (5x1), 10 (5x2), 15 (5x3), etc. A factor is a number that divides into another number without a remainder, or the different numbers multiplied together to get a given number, e.g. the factors of 24 are: 8 and 3, 4 and 6, 12 and 2, and 24 and 1. Working with multiples of 6 is one of the most common math concepts in amigurumi crochet pattern writing.

Multiples of 6

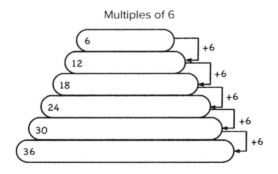

Multiples:
1 x 6 = 6, where 6 is a multiple of 6
2 x 6 = 12, so 12 is a multiple of 6

Factors:
1 x 6 = 6, where 1 and 6 are factors of 6
2 x 3 = 6, where 2 and 3 are factors of 6

Applying Factors in a Pattern

[1 sc, inc] repeat 6 times. (18 sts)

2, 3, and 6 are factors of 18

(a) The # of placeholders (separated by a comma) inside [..]
(b) The total # of stitches inside [..]
(c) Repeat x times

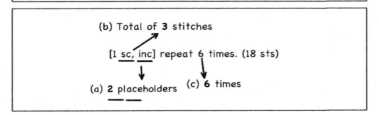

(b) Total of **3** stitches

[1 sc, inc] repeat 6 times. (18 sts)

(a) **2** placeholders   (c) **6** times

Applying Division in a Pattern

Round 2 [inc] repeat 6 times. (12 sts)

Round 3 [1 sc, inc] repeat 6 times. (18 sts)

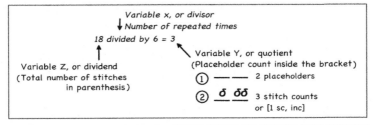

Variable x, or divisor
↓ Number of repeated times

18 divided by 6 = 3

Variable Z, or dividend
(Total number of stitches
in parenthesis)

Variable Y, or quotient
(Placeholder count inside the bracket)

① ──── 2 placeholders

② ᗡ ᗡᗡ 3 stitch counts
or [1 sc, inc]

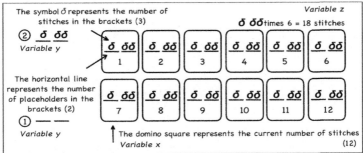

The symbol ᗡ represents the number of
stitches in the brackets (3)

② ᗡ ᗡᗡ
Variable y

The horizontal line
represents the number
of placeholders in the
brackets (2)

① ── ──
Variable y

Variable z

ᗡ ᗡᗡ times 6 = 18 stitches

ᗡ ᗡᗡ	ᗡ ᗡᗡ	ᗡ ᗡᗡ	ᗡ ᗡᗡ	ᗡ ᗡᗡ	ᗡ ᗡᗡ
1	2	3	4	5	6
ᗡ ᗡᗡ	ᗡ ᗡᗡ	ᗡ ᗡᗡ	ᗡ ᗡᗡ	ᗡ ᗡᗡ	ᗡ ᗡᗡ
7	8	9	10	11	12

The domino square represents the current number of stitches
Variable x   (12)

Pattern with Remainders and the Non-Evenly Divided

The patterns that are easier to follow and write are the ones in which the steps are consistently repeated in a round. The more complicated patterns are the ones with a mix of repeated steps within brackets (or parenthesis) and even some individual steps in a round. A combination of repeated and individual steps used in a round/row helps create those non-symmetrical, irregular shapes, so sometimes their complexity is warranted.

If you're designing a more complicated pattern without factors or multiples, make sure the number of stitches in the current round matches the total number of stitches from the previous round. Pattern testers can help catch those mathematical errors as well. Here are examples of patterns that combine repeats and single steps.

Example 1: A Pattern That Is Not Evenly Divided and with a Remainder of 1

Round 31   1 sc in each st. (5 sts)

Round 32   [1 sc, inc] repeat 2 times, 1 sc. (7 sts)

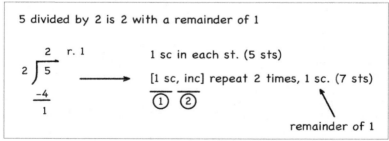

Example 2: A Pattern with a Combination of Repeated and Single Steps

Round 5   [1 sc, inc] repeat 6 times. (18 sts)

Round 6   1 sc, inc, [2 sc, inc] repeat 5 times, 1 sc. (24 sts)

---

18 sts in the first round = 18 placeholder count positions in the next round

[1 sc, inc] repeat 6 times. (18 sts)

1 sc, inc, [2 sc, inc] repeat 5 times, 1 sc. (24 sts)

① ①   ⑮   ①

1 + 1 + 15 + 1 = 18 placeholder counts

"All things are difficult before they are easy." Thomas Fuller.

The Power of Spiral Rounds

It's helpful to understand the circle pattern when designing. Knowing how to create circles in rounds or spiral rounds, not only spheres used for planets and doll heads, can also be applied to creating other 3D shapes like cones, cubes, and ovals. The key to creating different shapes is knowing when to increase/decrease and when to repeat the same stitches/rounds to determine the volume/size of the shape.

Let's start with the cone. When you visualize an amigurumi 3D triangle-like shape, the first thing that comes to mind is probably an ice cream cone. Now stretch your imagination. This 3D triangular shape can be the base form for spikes for dinosaurs and dragons, fangs for monsters or vampires, a horn for unicorns and narwhals, ears for cats, a beak for birds, or food shapes like Halloween candy corn or Japanese onigiri. So, what is the main difference between all these cone variations? It comes down to how pointy or elongated the cone is.

When creating a cone shape, the pattern typically starts at the point with the standard 6 sc in a magic ring for Round 1, just like when you start with the basic ball. Round 2, however, is where the change happens. Rather than forming the relative flatness of a circle, you want to create the pointed tip of the cone. How narrow or wide the cone ends up depends on how many increased stitches there are in the round. The more increased stitches in a round, the wider the shape becomes. The fewer increased stitches in a round, the more narrow the shape becomes.

For a very sharp, pointy cone, only 1 increase is needed in each round. More increases would be added to the round for a less pronounced or more obtuse cone. Remember to follow the counter increment/decrement formula for consistent increases/decreases in each round. Below is a comparison of different cone-size patterns:

Acute/Pointy (1 increase)		Medium (2 increases)		Obtuse (5 increases)	
Horns (Sharp and pointy)		Cat or fox ears		Stegosaurus spikes (Flat and wide)	
Rnd 1	6 sc in mr. (6 sts)	Rnd 1	6 sc in mr. (6 sts)	Rnd 1	6 sc in mr. (6 sts)
Rnd 2	5 sc, inc. (7 sts)	Rnd 2	[2 sc, inc] x2. (8 sts)	Rnd 2	1 sc, 5 inc. (11 sts)
Rnd 3	6 sc, inc. (8 sts)	Rnd 3	[3 sc, inc] x2. (10 sts)	Rnd 3	[1 sc, inc] x5, 1 sc. (16 sts)
Rnd 4	7 sc, inc. (9 sts)	Rnd 4	[4 sc, inc] x2. (12 sts)	Rnd 4	[2 sc, inc] x5, 1 sc. (21 sts)

"You create opportunities by performing, not complaining."
Muriel Siebert

Show Your Work

Remember when your math teacher would take points off your homework or test if you didn't show your work, even if you knew the answer to the math problem? The discipline to solve a math problem by manually writing it out applies to writing good crochet patterns. When figuring out the shapes you want to crochet, it is crucial to follow the same habits as what your math teacher made you do in school. Write out the steps.

Why is it so important to write out your crochet math steps? No teacher is grading you or looking over your shoulder. No one sees your scratchwork. It may sound a bit old school to take the time to write out your crochet math steps, but this step of the pattern writing process makes you a much better crochet designer and pattern writer in the long run.

One of the benefits of writing out the math is that it helps organize your thoughts. Writing out your steps and math helps you stay focused and also helps you remember important details that you might have otherwise overlooked. Even if you are writing the math steps to yourself, you're forcing your brain to visually process each step. If you make the pattern in your head and try to repeat it, you might miss something in the calculations or simply when translating from mind to paper.

It's frustrating when you're crocheting and you have to rip it all out because you made a counting mistake. Counting is an important part of crocheting. It's annoying when you can't remember where you left off in your counting. How do your loved ones know when you're deep in thought, concentrating on your project? They know not to bother you when you start counting out loud. Really loudly, really slowly. If we need to take this level of care with counting when we follow a pattern, then it makes good sense to use this same level of attention to detail when counting during the writing of a pattern.

Just remember that a lot of crochet designing is math, and math often means making mistakes and trying again until you get it right. You're going to make a lot of mistakes during the design process. Perfecting a masterpiece in one shot is pretty much impossible! So, it's important to write down your steps while crocheting during the design phase.

You'll save yourself time by taking notes and writing things down as you go, so you can look back at your steps instead of trying to remember what you did wrong. Writing out the math steps during the draft phase helps you check and confirm your formulas and counts. If you release a pattern with math mistakes, customers won't be happy they paid for it and you are unlikely to get repeat business. Crocheters love free patterns, but many are willing to buy patterns if they are good quality. Crocheters might be more likely to overlook a pattern with mistakes if it's free. If a paid pattern is poorly written, your customer might regret having spent money on it and not spend more money with you.

It's not just the potential loss of repeat business from one customer, though. If that one dissatisfied customer writes a poor review for errors or carelessness in your pattern/design, that will also dissuade new customers and prevent new sales. Therefore, write out the math on paper and check that your formulas and numbers all add up correctly. Take the time to show your work, even if it is a draft. It is well worth it.

Artist: Emi Creations by Chloe

3. STITCHES AND TECHNIQUES

The first step to learning crochet is how to properly control the crochet hook in one hand and yarn in the other hand, and then figuring out the basics of the slip knot, chain stitch, and single crochet. The must-know stitches in amigurumi crochet are the magic ring, single crochet, and the back and front loops. Other common stitches also include the slip stitch, half double crochet, double crochet, and so on, as these are the building blocks of crochet. You can, however, design an infinite number of amigurumi creations and variations with just the single crochet. The more stitches you know and master, the better the designer you will become. Similar to understanding the math concepts behind crochet patterns, understanding the mechanics behind stitches is equally important. Knowing different stitches can add special touches to your design, such as techniques, texture, and shape. Understanding the mechanics makes you better able to describe and demonstrate the steps in your pattern.

Back and Front Loops

Back loop only (BLO) stitches are fairly common in all types of crochet patterns. The back loop only version of a stitch is when you crochet into the loop furthest from you rather than inserting the hook into both "v" parts of the stitch. Working with the back loop creates a decorative line or ridge-like texture, but it's also quite versatile for special techniques and shortcuts. You've likely seen the back loop stitch in many patterns, but you probably never looked into how it's used for function rather than aesthetics. When you complete a row or round with back loops, what remains visible are the front loop stitches. You can then use special techniques on the remaining front loops.

One technique that becomes possible as a result of back loop stitches is the ability to join new yarn or attach separate pieces to the exposed front loops. It's easier to join parts into the loop than to sew them. If you find ways to avoid sewing when assembling limbs and body parts in amigurumi creations, mention it to buyers — it could be a selling point! Joining yarn to the loop gives it an "outer" layer look.

For example, you can use the front loop joining technique to crochet a scarf onto the main body of a holiday-themed bear, instead of sewing the scarf separately onto the bear. Using the front loop joining method avoids having to crochet pieces separately, set parts aside, and then sew them onto the main body later. It saves time, even yarn, but more importantly, it saves crocheters the frustration of assembling and sewing. Joining pieces or joining new yarn to the front loop stitches that remain from crocheting with back loop only stitches is a good technique to use in your work.

The use of back loop stitches also impacts the structure of the object. When you crochet into one loop and not both strands of the "v" stitch, this weakens the hold of the object. This point of weakness creates a crease or bend. A crease can alter a shape, which you can use in your design. For example, a creased edge can change a flat circle into a cylinder, with the back loop stitch outlining the edge or circumference of the object. This crease also works well for new rounds that need increasing or expansion, such as the brim of a hat.

The front loop only (FLO) stitch works the same way as the back loop stitch. The front loop stitch is when you crochet into the loop closest to you or the front of the "v" part of the stitch. The outline of the stitch is not visible from the front or outside. The ridge line is visible from the back side or inside. When joining yarn, you are left with the back loop to join to, and this creates a "crater" or an "inner layer" look.

Specialty Stitch Patterns

Knowing unique stitches is a great skill to have in your back pocket for crochet designing. There are so many unique stitches and styles to know and learn. Applying stitch patterns to your design work is mostly for looks. However, stitch patterns can occasionally be used for texture or to replace traditional shape patterns. Applying stitch patterns to your work also adds complexity to a basic design, making the end product and the process of crocheting it more interesting.

First come up with a basic design and write one pattern. Then, by adding unique stitches, you can easily create a new variation of the same design. Starting with one basic pattern, you can generate a second pattern, a third pattern, and so on, just by using different stitches! So, you'd start with one pattern to sell, but end up with multiple patterns with limited additional investment of time. The variations are endless.

For example, a simple amigurumi mermaid or owl pattern is with repeated rounds of single crochet. The crocodile stitch can be used to make patterns more interesting. For example, the crocodile stitch creates scales for the mermaid and feathers for the owl. Afterward, replace the crocodile stitch with the waffle stitch. The waffle stitch gives off a new texture. You've now created a new style with the same design and pattern with just the slightest alteration. Changing up the stitch style can make a big difference because then you can sell multiple patterns with barely more time than it took to write the first pattern!

The texture is not just about how it feels but also how it looks. Designing a sheep pattern can also be easily altered using different specialty stitches. For example, using chenille yarn, you can create a sheep with repeated single crochet rounds. The chenille fabric gives the sheep its soft-like texture. To crank this design up a notch, applying the loop stitch or the bobble stitch gives the sheep the appearance of a wool-like, crimped, curly texture. Your first sheep pattern is now a second pattern with a loop stitch, and the third pattern with a bobble stitch, but the shape structure stays the same. Specialty stitches can make something ordinary look unique and stand out.

Artists: Airali Design, Funny Rabbit Toys, Knot Monster, Magic Filament

Specialty stitch patterns can replace shape pieces as well. For example, the previous section mentioned the sphere and cone patterns to create vampire fangs or animal ears. The picot stitch (or the triangle pointed edge) can be used for accessory body parts rather than crocheting separate triangles or cone shapes. Another example is the bobble or puff stitch for a doll's nose or a bunny's tail instead of crocheting separate round body parts and then sewing the pieces together.

Trying out different stitch types can give your crocheting a whole new look and feel, and it's also a great way to learn new methods and techniques. A lot of people hate sewing pieces together when they make amigurumi. Shortcuts like the "no-sew" method can attract customers. Some customers might purchase the pattern, not for the design itself, but to learn how to avoid assembling and sewing for their other projects.

Additional Crochet Stitches

Symbol	Abbr.	Meaning
⌒	BLO	back loop only
⌣	FLO	front loop only
𝕠.𝕠	ch-3 picot	
⬭	3-hdc cluster/puff st/bobble	
⬭	5-dc popcorn	
⊺	FPdc	front post double crochet
⊺	BPdc	back post double crochet

Specialty Stitches Ideas

STITCH	STYLE
Basketweave	Design: Wicker basket-look (texture) *Suggested look for: Outline, scars*
Bobble, Popcorn, Puff	Design: Lump, or bumpy-look (3-D texture) *Suggested look for: Nose, beard, wool*
Chevron, Ripple	Design: Geometric, "v" style *Suggested look for: Zigzag, scar, color change*
Crocodile	Design: Scales, feather (texture) *Suggested look for: Leaf, fish, owl*
Fan	Design: Fan, feather (texture) *Suggested look for: Fan, earrings, owl*
Picot	Design: Small peaks for border edges *Suggested look for: Crown, fangs*
Shell	Design: Ocean wave style *Suggested look for: Ocean waves, Frankenstein Bride's hair, color change*
Waffle	Design: Geometric square, waffle-look (texture) *Suggested look for: Food*

Increases in the Same Stitch

Even if you only know a handful of basic stitches, you can create so many variations with just a sprinkle of imagination dust! Increasing in the same stitch can be used for a variety of designs, even if it is unclear at first what the stitch is for. The term increase implies "2 stitches to be completed in the next one stitch". However, the number of stitches in one stitch is not limited to just two.

Increasing just means adding more stitches in a round or row, but it plays a very important role in changing the item's structure and texture. When there are more new stitches in the stitch than space allows for, it starts to get crowded, creating a scrunching or rippling effect. This technique is used for the curly cue stitch and the ruffle stitch. For example, making an octopus's tentacles or a doll's hair curly comes down to putting a bunch of single or double crochets in the same stitch.

The ruffle stitch works the same way as the curly cue stitch. The frills or pleats become wavier as you crochet more into the same stitch. People usually think of ruffles as the frilly details on dresses and the edges of blankets and pillowcases. Many crochet patterns use a ruffle stitch on a doll's dress to make it frilly. The ruffle stitch can also be used to make less obvious things — that's where crochet knowledge and creativity come together! For example, the ruffle stitch method can create a "wrinkly" effect, such as the oozing brains of zombies, the head tops of leafy cabbages, or comfort foods like pie crust and lasagna. Bring on the creativity. The ruffle stitch isn't just for dolls anymore!

Artists: Knot Monster, Funny Rabbit Toys

Embroidery

Not that you need to pick up another hobby, but combining embroidery with crochet adds a new level of interest to your crochet designs. Adding embroidery into the crochet world has become a popular trend. Embroidery gives your amigurumi a finished look, and there are some shortcut techniques you can use to replace certain crochet stitches.

Crocheters are often concerned about the choking hazard risks of tiny parts. When adding eyes to dolls and stuffed animals, you can embroider lines for eyes, eyelids, and eyelashes instead of using safety eyes. You can make small buttons or polka dots using the French knot stitch instead of sewing magic ring circles or gluing felt on amigurumi toys. Check out some styles and research to see what embroidery techniques might help your crochet designs appeal to safety-conscious consumers and make your designs pop.

CHAPTER 3

P IS FOR POP

1. SKETCH AND SCRATCHWORK

Scribble Your Thoughts On Paper

You should be feeling pretty confident by now — knowing your crochet math and understanding the structure of crochet stitches. It's time to figure out what to design. You may already have one amazing idea in mind. But then, another idea and another idea pop into your head. Your brain suddenly gets flooded with this and that idea, and you start to lose track of which design you want to work on first. You're excited to start, but your head is all over the place. You're feeling anxious, and the sense of not knowing where to begin starts to set in. You then hit that reset button. You clear your head, and you feel motivated again.

~~~

There is one essential housekeeping item to keep in mind before you start designing: organization. Organizing your thoughts on paper is the best way to keep you from feeling overwhelmed and lost. Have a dedicated notebook to organize your thoughts so you can scribble and jot down all your ideas. You can have a section just for brainstorming ideas and another when you begin sketching your creation — even if it's messy. Choosing which crochet project you want to work on first might be challenging, but go ahead and pick one. Then concentrate on one pattern. Get one done before moving on to your next.

Even though you might be tempted to start writing the pattern and crocheting your creation, it's important to first write your ideas down on paper. There is a reason for carrying out this process. When too many fun ideas are overcrowding your head while also having outside distractions, you begin to experience cognitive overload. You are trying to work from memory, and the mental burden of keeping these ideas in your head can lead to mistakes. Taking the time to release your thoughts on paper provides you relief. This writing process allows you to externalize your thoughts so you don't have to rely on memory and prevents you from forgetting important information. When you write things down, your ideas are now documented somewhere and you don't have to work as hard to remember the finer details.

Another reason why it's crucial to put your ideas on paper is metacognition. Metacognition is the process of thinking. You think you sound eloquent and confident when you talk inside your head. But when you speak aloud, you realize your thoughts are not as clearly constructed. Now try talking in front of the mirror. You'll probably fumble with your words and begin losing your train of thought. The idea of talking inside your head versus talking aloud is just like transferring your thoughts on paper. This exercise is self-reflection on paper, and it forces you to think. By creating a free-flow outline, you can figure out the next steps in the planning process and realize steps and details you may not have considered.

Draw Like a Five-Year-Old

When hunting for crochet ideas on the web or social media, you might come across posts of crochet designers' amazing works of art, and not just of their finished amigurumi, but their actual drawings. Don't be intimidated by high quality design sketches that could be art in its own right. Even though drawing is a common step in design planning, it's optional. The drawing process is just one way to express your thoughts on paper. The purpose of the pencil-to-paper thought process is just that — the thought process. As long as you get your juices flowing, jotting words down on paper is sufficient for planning your design. You certainly don't have to draw like a professional artist, and no one besides you needs to see your sketches.

Should you wish to sketch out your designs, start doodling and see what you come up with. It's all about exercising the brain. Also, whether you know how to draw or not, utilizing various art mediums or materials like colored pencils or oil pastels can be used as another avenue to help get your creativity flowing. Applying colors to your drawings or even holding a different type of writing utensil allows your senses to explore sight and touch differently than if you took a pencil to draw your ideas.

The idea behind sketching your design is to help construct and prepare mental notes from thought to paper. Gathering your thoughts and writing them down will help you make better decisions as to what goes into your design. In addition, this process helps you better visualize what your likes and preferences are. As a result, your designs get better, and that in turn helps build your confidence as a designer and pattern writer.

Sometimes, when you're in the middle of working on your draft design, you may start to question yourself — your talent and entrepreneurial abilities — again. Having self-doubt is normal, but keep at it. Now that you have your outline, notes, and self-reminders laid out, along with a sketch on paper, you can quickly push away your incessant second-guessing and insecurities. And without realizing it, you've put out your own mini-fires. Instill this healthy practice of sketching out your thoughts on paper. You've got this!

Artist: Airali Design

"A person who never made a mistake never tried anything new."
Albert Einstein

2. FIND YOUR MUSE

You may have a few design ideas up your sleeve, but what if you run out of ideas? What if you have designer's block? What if you know how to write patterns but don't know what to design? Maybe you feel you're just not creative enough. How can crochet designers be so prolific when they can easily crank new amigurumi one after another, pattern after pattern?

"I can crochet, but how can I ever catch up with *them*?" If you feel defeated seeing all your favorite crochet designers publishing new blog posts week after week, don't give up yet! It's important to be inspired by crochet designers and aspire to be like them, but not at the expense of thinking less of yourself or your talents. Remember that this is *your* journey, so push away any negative thoughts and keep going. The good news is there's a simple strategy to easily come up with ideas. The truth is, ideas can come from anything and anywhere. Ideas don't have to come out of thin air. You can look all around you for them.

Expand Your Horizons

Rather than designing something from scratch, take inspiration from others and the objects around you. It can be frustrating to start from a blank slate. Instead of coming up with something completely new, try grabbing ideas from what already exists and combining them with your own tweaks and improvements.

Anything that interests you can be inspiration. The easiest and quickest place to gather ideas is on the internet. There's a wealth of information, sometimes to the point of overload, when browsing the internet. There are so many other hidden gems you can browse through: children's books, your favorite arts and crafts shop, the greeting cards aisle at the grocery store, a candy store, or a specialty gift store. If you're into crocheting cutesy, kawaii objects (meaning cute in Japanese), you can take ideas from stickers, cartoon characters, comic books, toys, or even memes and emojis. There are so many places you may have never thought to look for inspiration.

Know What's Trending

An efficient way to find inspiration is to see what's trending. Searching for ideas from what's popular can also be a very lucrative strategy! Though the subject or topic may only be short-lived, you can milk the opportunity before time passes when the trend is long gone or forgotten. What's popular or trending can be something other than a new Disney or Marvel character. Unexpected ideas are surprisingly the ones that go viral.

Remember the Bernie Sanders crochet doll that went viral soon after the 2021 US Presidential Inauguration? Originally taking inspiration from a meme, crochet designer Tobey King sold a finished doll of the Vermont Senator for $20,000 (donated to charity) and sold over 30,000 copies (as of January 2021) for this one pattern alone! Many other crochet designers jumped on the same bandwagon to grab inspiration from this monumental event and the fact that Bernie's curmudgeon face and mittens went viral.

Another event that made headlines was the 2022 Russian invasion of Ukraine. Putting political opinions aside, crochet designers took this opportunity to increase awareness and drive in business by designing anything related to Ukraine. There are hundreds of crochet patterns for doves and sunflowers, and things as simple as blue and yellow striped heart patterns, as these symbolize peace or represent the flag colors of Ukraine.

Seek and You Will Find

Inspiration can also extend beyond things in the now. For example, historical, religious, or cultural references can trigger inspiration. You can also consider inspirations that are timeless. Many designs never change or grow old. Ideas can come from your favorite nursery rhyme, fairy tales, myths, or folk-lore. Inspiration can come from the five senses, emotions, and personality traits, too. Crochet ideas sometimes come naturally on your own, but sometimes, effort must be intentional. Just create for the sake of creating! Ideas and productivity can happen when we just do and don't think. Being creative also means thinking outside the box, looking for that great idea that hasn't been discovered yet, and making new discoveries.

"Have no fear of perfection — You'll never reach it." Salvador Dali

Embrace the Dark Side

It's human nature to gravitate toward things that are considered beautiful. But what is beauty exactly? When people think of nature, they often equate beauty to nature and associate nature with serenity, peace and quiet, blue skies, and rainbows. But, on the flip side, nature can also be dark, scary, chaotic, and destructive.

When considering ideas on what to design, inspiration can be something other than colorful, cutesy, or even symmetrical. Attractiveness doesn't have to mean happiness. Likewise, inspiration doesn't all have to be sunshine and roses. Beauty can also signify sadness, nostalgia, or even fright. In the non-traditional sense of beauty, particularly in amigurumi, inspiration can be grotesque, strange, or distorted.

Art is subjective. Subconscious biases, such as beauty bias, influence people's decision-making constantly. Biases apply to crochet selling and buying as well. Something that you don't find attractive can be considered quite attractive to others. What you think is ugly may be beautiful to some. Designing unconventional or unique ideas can be an untapped financial opportunity to consider. Embrace new ideas that may be unfamiliar to you. Experiment with shock factor in your designs.

For example, think of fun crochet ideas that are scary or spooky, such as Halloween creations. Halloween is a very lucrative time of the year for crochet entrepreneurs! Embroidering a red streak scar across Frankenstein's forehead or an ear-to-ear grin across a skeleton's face gives a bit of a shock factor. Frankenstein isn't just a green monster, but a monster with a noticeable scar on his face. A Halloween skeleton isn't just a string of skinny bones but a creature of the night with empty eye sockets and a creepy smile. These characters look endearing in a grotesque way.

Many crocheters may be more accustomed to working on unicorn and turtle projects throughout most of the year. Still, when Halloween comes around, crocheters prepare weeks in advance to begin working on bats, creepy crawlies, poison apples, and skulls. Think of steampunk and goth genres. They're dark, mysterious, and wildly popular niches. Some designers have found great success focusing on the non-cutesy, non-kawaii-themed genres.

Elements of Design

Line		Strokes to imply movement. (Vertical, horizontal, curves, diagonal, zigzag.)
Form		Shape with 3-dimension (length, width, height).
Space		The illusion of depth (negative space).
Texture		How an object feels. How an object appears to feel.
Shape		Connected lines, 2-dimension.
Color		Use of light, hue.
Value		Lightness (tint) and darkness (shade) of color.

3. INSPIRED BY VS. PLAGIARISM

Inspiration can come from anywhere, anything, or even anyone. More cases than not, there are a lot of crochet designers claiming and selling their designs and patterns as their own when one could question the likeness and integrity of the artwork. Is the design a replica of someone else's work? How much is too much likeness? It's one thing to be inspired by someone else's art, but it's another thing to blatantly copy it. But even if one's artwork doesn't have all the similarities of someone else's, is one's inspiration still a possible case of plagiarism, or even worse — copyright infringement? Depending on the design and the intent of one's inspiration, one could fall into the gray area of plagiarism.

What is plagiarism? First off, plagiarism is a matter of ethics — what is morally right or wrong — not a matter of law. Plagiarism is when you pass off someone else's creation as your own. Simply put, you are stealing someone else's work and taking credit for it. Plagiarism doesn't just stop at copying word for word or designing something that is identical. Plagiarism is much bigger than a simple copy and paste. The intent to copy a design with the slightest alteration can still be an act of plagiarism. Paraphrasing written patterns or altering the looks of another crochet design can be a gray area for plagiarism, assuming you are taking that same idea or intent from another work.

Because shapes and patterns make up crochet designs, it is easy for designs to have similar looks and outcomes, which can often make it hard to determine whether there was plagiarism. There are only so many ways to write a written pattern for a ball, a cube, or curly cue stitches. Designing a common object and then comparing it to one by a different designer might result in two objects nearly indistinguishable from one another.

If you compare one amigurumi octopus to another octopus, it's quite possible both designs will look like one another. The written patterns will likely be written out the same way because there is a standard way of making the tentacles and a limited variety of body shapes that tend to be used. Imagine the body structure of a doll or a gnome. One gnome's pattern to another gnome's pattern will probably be quite similiar, likewise one doll to another doll. Something as simple as a scarf is made up of rows, crocheting back and forth. The chances of finding hundreds of nearly identical patterns of a simple scarf are very likely.

Although there is a possibility that crochet designs and patterns could be perceived as plagiarism because they can be easily replicated, this shouldn't stop you from pursuing your interests in making your designs and selling your patterns. Think of all the math teachers writing out lesson plans for the class. How many ways can you explain and write without having other math instructors not teach the same way? It's difficult for crochet designs and written patterns not to have similarities and resemblances, especially when they are for items that we all see and expect to look a standard way. According to the US Copyright Office, crochet patterns fall under "works of visual art," where patterns can be copyrighted but not stitches. If you're confident with your designs and writing pattern style and your intent is genuine, try not to worry too much and continue to pursue your interests in crochet design.

Some crocheters might try to copy other designers' work on purpose, but this is not your intent at all! It is completely okay to be inspired by other people's work, and genuinely want to share your skills and artwork with the crochet world. Go ahead and be inspired by others! If you are honest with yourself, don't let the fear of possible "copying" stop you.

It Never Hurts to Ask

Think back to when you wrote essays and research papers in school. One of the requirements when writing a paper is to cite all your references and include a bibliography. Adding the reference section can be an annoying part of the essay writing process. What's the point of having a reference section when most people don't even look at it?

The purpose of citing your sources is to let readers know your words and thoughts came from somewhere else. The same goes for crochet. If your inspiration came from another designer, the honorable thing to do is to acknowledge the designer. Be respectful and give credit where it's due. The crochet business may be competitive and saturated because it is a commodity market, but a hobby like crochet shouldn't be a cutthroat business. Crochet is a favorite pastime for many, so it should be enjoyable and non-threatening.

If a designer inspired your design, contact that designer and ask if it is okay to credit her when you sell your pattern. Be honest and transparent with the other designer, and let her know your artwork and writing are completely your own, and it was her work that inspired your creation.

Out of courtesy, let the other designer know you would like to acknowledge her business name when you promote and sell your pattern. Make sure your work has distinct enough features that separate your design from hers. Send a photo of your finished work to the other designer, showing there are differences as well as some similarities. The other designer can see how they may have inspired your work and hopefully won't feel threatened or get the impression that you are claiming their work as your own. The other designer will likely not object, especially if your marketing and publication efforts also mention their name or business.

It is also possible that the other designer started their crochet business long before yours. So, telling them that you want to acknowledge them may not be a big deal. If they have a flourishing business and a loyal customer base, your reference to them is unlikely to impact their sales at all. If the other designer already has an established business, you may indirectly bring more traffic to them. They may be flattered and even wish you luck in your new endeavors. This situation, of course, is the optimal outcome for your inspiration source.

However, if the designer you are inspired by says no, hopefully with a reasonable explanation for the rejection, ask yourself why you may disagree with their response. For example, is your design too much of a likeness to the other designer's work? Don't beat yourself up for reaching out, being transparent, and asking the other designer for permission. You're an honest person, and you want to do right by other artists, especially the designer who inspired you.

Sometimes life doesn't turn out the way you planned, or at least how it played out in your head. So, what do you do now? If the designer registered their work with the government, legal action can be pursued due to copyright infringement. And even if the other designer never officially filed paperwork with the government, technically, all published patterns are still copyrighted. Though disheartening, it is better to be safe than sorry not to move forward with this project and instead move on with another design.

However, it is essential to remember that an idea or inspiration cannot be copyrighted. Suppose your artwork is distinct enough from the other designer, and your written pattern is clearly yours. In that case, confirm with friends and others who are unbiased whether your design appears sufficiently unique. If the answer is yes, then be confident about selling your pattern.

What's All the Hype About

A bigger concern here is not about copying or being inspired by another crochet designer's work, but about copying designs from mainstream art that clearly has copyright protection. So, what does copyright mean anyway? Plainly put, it is when one has the right to copy. If you intend to make money from your crochet work, shy away and steer clear from designing things from what you see in recent movies and books.

You may be tempted, but avoid Disney, Marvel, and other known characters. You're probably asking yourself, "Why do so many crocheters make and sell all these fun characters — Hello Kitty, Spiderman, Pusheen, Minion, and Grogu? I'm sure they're profiting from these characters. Why can they do it and not me?" Well, you can. It's pretty easy to make a red and white ball with a black line in the middle and then attach a white circle to create a Pokemon ball. The question you need to ask yourself is not *can* you do it, but *should* you be doing it, especially if it means possibly violating copyright laws? What are your true intentions for designing and writing patterns in the first place? Is it to share your love of crochet and designs with others, or is your desire to profit from the foundational work of others?

If you've been to sporting events, you often see street vendors selling sports team merchandise: shirts, caps, and beanie hats. Many are bootleg, and those vendors most likely don't have licenses to sell. They do it anyway because they believe they won't get caught by these big corporations. The same goes for the crochet business. The chances of getting caught may be slim, especially for designers residing outside the US or in countries with less stringent copyright laws.

Truth be told, minimal law enforcement sometimes sways one's ethical compass. Is it okay to do something wrong or unethical if you know you're not going to get caught? Think about driving above the speed limit. Most people drive above the speed limit when there are no cops around. But once you see that speed trap from a distance, you immediately take your foot off the gas pedal and follow that number on the highway sign. Sometimes you follow the rules not because it's the right thing to do but because you know authority is watching you, and you fear getting caught. You never know who is looking at your content online.

Lastly, crochet designs aren't just limited to art but also the likeness of a celebrity or a well-known person. The likeness of a public figure is called the "right of publicity." An artist cannot exploit the likeness of someone without their permission, physical or personal character, even if the known figure is no longer living. For example, you may have seen the Bernie Sanders and Queen Elizabeth II crochet dolls or other public figures on social media. Technically, the designer should ask permission to use the person's likeness if they plan to profit from their high profile status. However, this law depends on where the crochet designer resides. Not just laws in different countries, but even within the US, some States have their own image rights and other intellectual property related protection laws.

Often the case, copyright enforcement or similarly related laws generally tend to be confusing. When in doubt, be honest with yourself. Either do your research or move on to another great idea of yours.

Stick to the Classics

If you have the itch to design and write patterns in a niche that focuses on popular characters and known figures, it's safer to stick with the "classics," where copyright laws have expired or are in the public domain. According to US copyright laws, any works published before 1924 are free to use. Works published between 1924 and 1977 are protected for 95 years from the work's publication date, and if works were created but not published before 1978, copyright still lasts for the author's lifetime, plus an additional 70 years. Bottom line, if it's at least a century old, you're probably okay to design away.

Designing characters in the public domain can still be tricky. Many book characters, for example, have been turned into movies, remakes, and even spin-offs. Examples include storybooks and characters like Alice in Wonderland and Wizard of Oz. These books are considered classic novels and are in the public domain, but if the movies and not the actual books inspired your crochet designs and patterns, then your designs may be in question.

Using the Wizard of Oz example, Dorothy's shoes play an essential role in the story plot. Dorothy wears silver shoes in the original books, but the cultural reference is her wearing red, ruby slippers, taken from Judy Garland's 1939 classic film. The movie producers purposely gave Dorothy red shoes because Hollywood introduced color for the first time when movies back in the day were originally all black and white. The producers wanted the movie to have as many bright, flashy colors as possible. The intentional use of crocheting a Dorothy doll with red slippers is technically under copyright protection, but not if your design of Dorothy wears silver shoes.

Other examples include Disney movie characters. Many stories from Disney originate from classic fairy tales of the Grimm Brothers and Hans Christian Andersen. If you're a crocheter of dolls, you are well aware of Disney's Cinderella, Snow White, The Princess and Frog, Rapunzel, The Little Mermaid, and Frozen. These princess and heroine stories come from classic fairy tales. Even Mulan and Pocahontas come from actual historical events.

Should you wish to design and sell princess doll patterns, make sure the likeness and intention are not from Disney but from the original stories that are no longer in copyright status. You're probably wondering why many crochet designers continue to sell these character patterns. The designers may have stayed true to the book characters, not Disney's. Or maybe, they circumvented copyright technicalities by not explicitly mentioning Disney and used generic descriptions of the characters when selling their patterns. Or they might just be lucky and haven't been caught, yet!

When in doubt, check your country's copyright laws, consult a lawyer for the most accurate and current information, or move on to your next design without the potential drama. Should you release patterns on online shopping platforms, the company might have an obligation to follow copyright laws. Should a viewer or outside party believe your design infringes upon a copyright or right of publicity license, Etsy, for example, immediately notifies you and automatically removes the content from your site. You, as the designer, also have the right to contest this dismissal with the other party outside of Etsy. To play it safe with what you choose to design and make, read up on your books and history to confirm where your inspiration originates.

"If you can't do great things, do small things in a great way."
Napoleon Hill

---

4. MIX AND MATCH

Inspiration can be pulled from multiple sources and then combined and meshed into an original, new design. The opportune words here are *combined and meshed*: the mix and match opportunity to put multiple shapes and patterns together with a single commonality or a central theme. Mixing and matching is a great strategy to keep in mind when designing. This provides an easy way to develop ideas of the same patterns with minimal changes.

Artist: Aradiya Toys

"The true sign of intelligence is not knowledge but imagination."
Albert Einstein

Mr. Potato Head Method

Do you remember the popular toy Mr. Potato Head back in the day? Mr. Potato Head is a toy with a central body part, the "head." Detachable body parts are then attached to the head. If you think about it, attaching different parts to the main body is commonly used in crochet design. You can create multiple styles using one primary pattern: an X-in-1 pattern. Not only is this method an effective way to create multiple patterns, but your market campaigning can also benefit from this strategy.

Have you ever gone shopping and seen a sign that reads "2 for the price of 1?" The catchy phrase is an attention grabber, as people's minds think they're getting a good deal. Whether the item is a good bargain or not, it attracts potential customers to see what's being sold. This marketing tactic can also work for selling crochet patterns. Catchy phrases like "3 in 1 pattern" or "pattern bundle" can draw window shoppers to check out your patterns. They are more likely to buy your pattern, save it in their shopping cart, or at least flag it as a favorite.

The strategy is to have the same crochet pattern for the main body and different patterns for the other components that make up the finished object. For example, you can create any animal with a similarly shaped torso and head by repeating the same pattern for its torso and head. Imagine a bunny, cat, or lion. The distinction between these animals is their different body parts: the ears, nose, and tail. These body parts will then have different patterns to complete the animals. For example, a bunny has long, floppy ears; a cat has triangular, pointy ears; and a lion has round ears and a mane. You can use the same pattern for the torso and head, and simply write different patterns for the limbs.

Mismatch Juxtaposition Method

The most fun and unique designs are the ones with the most contrast or the least expected combinations of shapes. Take, for instance, Mr. Potato Head, a potato with a caricature-like face. The idea of putting body parts onto a random object like a vegetable root is unlike anything imagined. It's not like the traditional dolls or animals with pieces put together — but a *potato*? This is non-traditional thinking at its best!

Combining something familiar with something completely random is something to keep in mind. Keep a common theme for the primary shape as the main pattern and alternate the supporting parts to merge the pieces to create a finished design. That's the great thing about designing and imagination!

The strategy is to find everyday, mundane objects and merge them with unlikely objects.

An example can be a turtle or a snail and replacing the shell with random objects like a house, a pumpkin, a flower, or a birthday cake instead. Another random idea can be the ice cream on a cone. Rather than a 3-tiered stacked ice cream, replace the top tier with an animal head. It may initially look odd to consider combining food and an animal head, but the mismatch of random objects is intentional. The mismatching of half-and-half objects creates a unique shock factor that catches people's attention. Think of mythical creatures like a mermaid or a centaur where humans are half fish or half horse. Another random idea can be the ordinary hot dog. Rather than crocheting the meat between the bun, crochet a Dachshund (or wiener) dog or a long worm instead.

Artists: Funny Rabbit Toys, Funny Rabbit Toys, Emi Creations by Chloe

Another idea is utilizing holiday theme designs. For example, place a black cat's head with a witch hat on top of a pumpkin, a cauldron, or a mug of hot cocoa with marshmallows. These ideas of unlike pairings of random objects to create an entirely new object give you endless opportunities on what you can come up with. The crochet world of imagination doesn't have to make sense; whimsical creations come to life as long as you are making crochet fun!

Color Changes Method

One way to come up with variations of the same pattern is to alter the design of a same shaped pattern with the color change method. An example would be writing a pattern for a single-colored subject, such as a black cat. The following pattern would be using the same shaped pattern with alternating colors between rounds to create stripes, such as a striped tabby cat. You can now sell two patterns: one for a black cat and another for a tabby cat. It's the same pattern but in different colors. Another example is changing colors to create irregularly formed shapes and spots throughout the pattern. Continuing with the amigurumi cat example, this would be creating the same shaped pattern for different types of cats, such as the calico, tuxedo, and tabby.

Artists: Littlehand Crochet, JuliaKa Pattern

Another same shaped pattern with different colors is to alter the subject, such as an animal species. Imagine a grizzly bear and a panda bear. It's the exact shape. It's still a bear but in different colors. The total number of stitches and the shape of the primary object don't change; it's the color in the pattern that changes. For mapping complex color changes, a helpful online tool is Stitch Fiddle.

Artists: Amiguruku, Storyland Amis, Audrey Lilian Crochet

Using the same shape pattern can also have a completely altered physical appearance just by applying color changes to the pattern. Using the same shaped pattern with altered colors doesn't have to be related subjects, such as designing one cat for another cat or one bear for another bear. For example, a sphere pattern can create various objects. That same sphere ball can make a Halloween eyeball, a hacky sack ball, or the planet Earth. A cone-shaped pattern can make an erupting volcano, an ice-capped mountain, a giant candy corn, or an onigiri. Imagine stacked ice cream scoops. The same shaped pattern can be used to create a snowman. Now imagine turning the same shaped pattern sideways. That same pattern can be used to create a plump caterpillar. Utilizing one shape for a pattern and applying different colors can turn one creation into several new creations.

Artist: Airali Design, Lucy Magic Pattern, Monster Hook

Common Groupings and Themes Method

Another mix and match idea is to design a collection of individual finished objects with a similar theme or a common grouping. You can crochet different types of fruits: apples, oranges, grapes, strawberries, cherries, and bananas. Or, you can crochet planets in the solar system, an astronaut, an alien, and a rocket ship for the theme of outer space.

From the designer's perspective, this strategy may be more time-consuming as you'll have to invest the time to design and write individual patterns for objects that may not have similar shapes or designs. From a customer's perspective, however, this may be the biggest bang for the buck for them since they'll be purchasing a collection of different patterns.

Of course, you can sell the patterns individually, but selling them as a collection of patterns is a great selling strategy. Though many small-sized amigurumi patterns can be found online for free, customers may be attracted to purchasing a collection of themed or grouped patterns rather than frustratingly searching and hunting online for single patterns. In addition, some customers like the convenience of having patterns pre-selected and bundled together as one purchase. Data shows 67% of consumers are willing to pay a premium for convenience.

Artist: Knot Monster

Another idea is to combine both the mismatch and common theme design methods. Take, for example, the zodiac or horoscope. You can write patterns for each horoscope sign and make this a collection of different patterns. However, you can also use a primary object, such as a doll or a dog, and then design 12 different headpieces representing each zodiac symbol. Rather than designing a full-body Scorpio (or scorpion); a full-body Sagittarius (or centaur); a full-body Pisces (or a pair of fish); and so on, design a primary pattern for the main body that can be repeated 12 times, and alter the body parts that represents the different zodiacs.

In addition, there are the 12-month astrological signs in Western culture as well as the 12-year cycle of animals in certain Asian cultures. You can take this opportunity to create 24 potential sets of zodiac designs. There are also various gemstones, flowers, and seasons that represent each month of the year. By following a thread of common themes, you can create an endless collection of amigurumi based on holidays or other events, especially if they overlap with cultures around the world.

Strike a Pose Method

Another mix and match approach is to design a set of different poses of the same object. For example, you can create a collection of cats in different positions, such as a cat standing on all fours, a cat with its front paws stretched out or tilting its head. The majority of the body parts will still have the same pattern shape. The slight tweak in the pattern is where/how the limbs need to be placed differently to achieve the poses. Another example can be a doll in different yoga positions. Or, rather than designing just a doll with two legs and two arms to the side of the body, you can design a doll in different positions, such as an angel lowering its head and hands folded in prayer or a kneeling position.

Artist: oche pots

When figuring out how to design common amigurumi objects, see what the common poses are. From there, add your twist in a new or different position that makes your design stand out from other crochet designers. Customers repeatedly see the same type of amigurumi pose or structure. You can create and design an object in a commonly posed position as one pattern and then create another object with a different pose for a second pattern. Again, this is an opportunity to sell not one pattern but two patterns just by tweaking the positioning of crochet parts.

You can also look beyond the stance or body position and consider altering the design of the face or facial structure. For example, rather than embroidering a typical smile, create an add-on to the face, such as a tongue sticking out. People are so used to seeing smiling dolls. Stand apart from your competitors and embroider a grumpy face or frown instead. Rather than attaching beads for the eyes, embroider a wink. Keep things interesting by adding contrast or subtle differences that make your products unique. It's about making your designs stand out from other designers.

Artists: Airali Design, Curious Papaya, Curious Papaya

5. COLORS OF THE RAINBOW

Some people have a natural eye for picking and choosing the right colors. For people a bit more artistically challenged, color theory can help you understand the relationship of colors, color mixing, and, more importantly, the psychology of colors. This isn't an exact science, but more of a guide to help you decide which color to use when designing.

Knowing how to mix colors together makes your designs look better to viewers. You want your potential customers to respond to your crochet designs in a way that makes them take a second and third look without needing to depend on background accessories when taking photos of your creations. It's your designs, not your photography skills, that should attract buyers. Colors can strike up certain moods. As the designer and seller, you want the best matched colors combined to catch the crochet shopper's immediate attention to like and ultimately purchase your patterns.

The Color Wheel

The first lesson in color theory often references the color wheel, created by the mathematician Isaac Newton. The color wheel is read like a map or clock, where the colors of the rainbow are placed in the order of the light spectrum. The colors are divided into 12 sections. Placed in rainbow order (red, orange, yellow, green, blue, indigo, and violet (ROYGBIV)), the general rule of thumb is that the primary colors are separated from one another at equilateral triangle positions.

Red is at 12 o'clock, yellow is at 4 o'clock, and blue is at 8 o'clock. Primary colors, red, yellow, and blue, are considered the purest form of natural light colors. Then mixing two primary colors, you get the secondary colors of purple, orange, and green. Tertiary colors are the other colors that reside on the color wheel, where the primary and secondary colors are then mixed to make up the third level of colors, and so on.

To choose which yarn colors work best together, the basic concept of matching colors is to look at the different "dials" of color from across the color wheel. For example, opposite colors of one bright and one dark color sit across each other on the color wheel. The paired colors are considered complementary colors. The recommended matching of three can be combined by taking the respective equilateral triangle positions on the color wheel. Or, you can use 4 colors by picking ones that form a rectangle, which is called the tetradic color scheme. An example of mix and match colors with this method are red, green, blue-violet, and yellow-orange. Using the color wheel as a guide helps designers harmoniously combine colors in a more organized way. Many free software apps, such as Canva, can help make color choices easy.

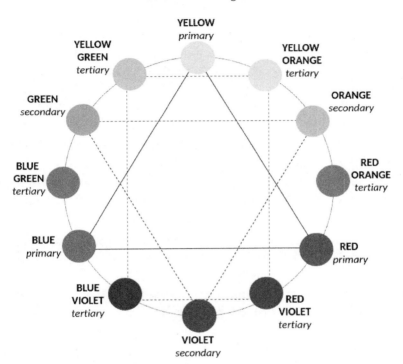

Color Wheel Diagram

Colors Provoke Emotions

Because color can play on human emotion, color can influence one's purchasing decision. Therefore, you want to be deliberate with your color choices when designing. Color choosing is based on the temperature in science and temperament in psychology. Looking at the color wheel, the purple, blue, and green color ranges are "cool" in temperature, as opposed to the red, orange, and yellow colors; these colors are "warm" in temperature.

People associate blue and green with soothing nature. These colors have a calming effect on the subconscious mind. More vibrant colors, like reds and oranges, bring attention and alert the eye. The blue and green scenery relaxes the mind when people think of the ocean, forest, and mountains. The sense of calmness and ease is why these colors give off far less of a reaction than the more eye-catching, sharp colors like reds and oranges. At a subconscious level, orange and red colors are associated with sensuality, excitement, fear, anger, and happiness. When people observe the colors red and orange in nature, this is the color of fire, hot lava, or a predatory animal like the tiger.

If you had to pick between a pale green apple and a bright red apple, which would you choose? People usually go for the red apple because it's more eye-catching. Whether you prefer Granny or Honeycrisp apple better — the sight is what matters, not the taste. Be deliberate with your color choices.

When designing something as simple as an amigurumi worm or snake, choose yarn colors like bright green, orange, or egg yolk yellow rather than light yellow or brown-green to catch people's attention. Though one would see a camouflaged worm or snake on the side of the road or backyard, avoid the brown yarn and use a fun color yarn instead. Customers will be more attracted to your designs if you use colors that pop rather than colors that blend into the surroundings.

Green with Envy

Many crocheters like to scroll through patterns online. Some look for a new project to work on, without knowing what they want to make. And some are laser-focused, knowing precisely what project to work on next. As a seller, you need to capture people's attention quickly, as you only have a split second to keep them interested in your pattern. Fingers crossed, you want the crochet shopper to click that "like" or "buy now" button. If people don't have a reaction, they're not going to look or buy. It's better to go with bolder, brighter colors rather than subtle or soft colors when designing.

Have you ever watched a home fixer-upper or a home selling show on TV? A lot of these home-selling shows go for bold colors when they repaint the walls. Now compare this to the real world when you go to an open house. Do you prefer neutral, off-white colors or bold colors for wall paint when you're looking to buy or rent a place? People usually go for the more neutral colors when buying a place, so it can easily blend in with their furniture, not a wall paint color that stands out on its own.

So why do television shows pick loud colors then, if, in reality, people prefer more toned-down colors? What you see on television is just for show. The intense colors are intended to catch the TV watcher's attention. However, what you see on TV probably differs from what you envision in real life. Just like posting photos of your designs, it's about catching the buyer's attention as quickly as possible.

Colors also impact consumer behavior, so focus on picking intense, stimulating colors that entice impulse buyers over passive window shoppers. Colors can affect potential customers' reactions to making a purchase, as well as how quickly they make a purchase. The longer the person has to think about buying something, the less likely the person will buy it.

When consumers see colors that are loud and vibrant, their perceptions of those colors also affect their perceptions of the brand. Since color is linked to beauty and emotions, there is a correlation between beauty bias and affinity bias. The consumer's subconscious mind has already prejudged how they feel about a product and a brand. Focus not on the colors you may like, but on colors that draw in customers. Be intentional with your color choices when selling your designs. It's about using common perceptions of colors and consumer biases to grab the attention of your potential pattern buyers.

A World That Revolves Around Diversity

In addition to applying color theory, it's helpful to be mindful and observant of what's around you. Color is often associated with nature, but color can also be associated with culture and trends. If you're designing items related to special events, choose colors according to the culture. However, it's good to keep in mind that holidays and notable events are also celebrated around the world. Just because one culture celebrates with certain colors doesn't mean all cultures do.

Artist: oche pots

The New Year is often celebrated with the colors black and gold in Western culture, associated with a final farewell to the past year. The song Auld Lang Syne is sung not only for New Year but also at funerals in Western culture. New Year is also celebrated in other parts of the world but with different themes and colors. For example, many countries in Asia use red for Lunar New Year to bring luck and wealth to the new year.

Another cultural color difference is the color white. White symbolizes purity in many Western cultures and is often used for weddings and baby christenings. On the other hand, white is associated with death in many Asian cultures, and is often worn at funerals. It's important to be mindful of your target audience, but that doesn't mean focusing only on one group over the other; you can still easily market to multiple cultures. A strategy would be to showcase two of the same design but with colors that reflect two different cultures. Just be mindful of how colors are selected. Colors may have different meanings and symbolism in various cultures.

COLOR	CULTURE AND MEANING
Red	Western: Excitement, danger, love, passion, Valentine's Eastern: Luck, happiness, celebration *Psychology: Stimulates brain wave activity, increases heart rate*
Orange	Western: Creativity, Autumn, Halloween Eastern: Abundance, good fortune *Psychology: Rejuvenates*
Yellow	Western: Hope, spontaneity, positivity Eastern: Auspicious, royalty, courage *Psychology: Energizes, relieves depression, improves memory*
Green	Western: Luck, new beginnings, money, Spring, St. Patrick's Eastern: Eternity, health, peace *Psychology: Soothes, relaxes, heals*
Blue	Western: Loyalty, faith, inspiration Eastern: Tranquility, healing, tranquility, Spring *Psychology: Calms, lowers blood pressure*
Indigo, Violet, Purple	Western: Royalty, wealth, fame, imaginative Eastern: Love, strength, royalty *Psychology: Protects, brings confidence*

A World That Evolves Around Inclusion

In recent years, many companies have emphasized diversity and inclusion as part of branding efforts. Consumers may find this admirable when companies embrace all representations of the population.

It's important to recognize all human beings, and it's a win-win for businesses big and small to use this as a marketing strategy. If you're a crochet doll designer, consider designing dolls of different skin tones, hair colors, and even hair textures and styles. Our society's reflection includes physical character-istics like race and skin color, hair and eye color, and body size, but also sexual orientation and people with physical and developmental disabilities. Utilizing colors that symbolize and celebrate differences in people and beliefs can also be used for marketing campaigns. Examples include designing pink hearts and ribbons for breast cancer survivors or using rainbow col-ors to celebrate the LGBTQ+ community. It's not just a way to attract a broader swath of customers, but also an opportunity to build goodwill, an invaluable asset for the positive branding of your crochet business.

Being open to broad representation helps grow your business. Put aside any biases or political and religious differences when building your crochet business. Everyone is entitled to their opinions. If consumers like what you're designing and selling, they'll buy from you. If people don't like what you're selling, they'll just move on. It's important to be kind to others and respect each other's cultures, beliefs, and differences.

CHAPTER 4

R IS FOR REPORT FORMAT

"It doesn't matter how slow you go, as long as you don't stop."
Confucius

1. LAYOUT

The Lay of the Land

Whether this is your first time writing a pattern or the tenth time, it's good to work from an existing pattern. Using an existing pattern as a template can save time because the format is already laid out. You don't have to start from a blank page, and you can use it as a guide to help you decide what information to include. Plus, overriding an existing pattern's text can make it easier to write out your own pattern sentences.

Different crochet designers may have their own writing style, but they all use a similar format structure. After following and reading through enough patterns, you should know which writing and format styles you like and dislike. It's best to reference one or two existing patterns to help you through your writing pattern process. Ultimately, it all comes down to the actual pattern instructions.

Some sections of a written pattern are more useful than others, similar to how a book is structured. A book usually contains a table of contents and a bibliography, but by no means do they convey the quality of how well-written the book is or how accurate the content is. Whether a book is good or not comes down to the chapters between the table of contents and bibliography. Written crochet patterns follow a similar practice. Some of the elements might not be as useful, but this is your chance to make sure every section of the document matters, not just the pattern section. Written patterns traditionally include the following sections:

- The first page, or cover page, often includes a full-size photo of the finished project, along with a title of the pattern and the crochet company or designer's name.

- The second and third pages include:
  - Difficulty skill level
  - Materials and supplies needed for the project
  - Measurement or sizing of the project once completed
  - Recommended hook size and yarn gauge
  - Crochet abbreviations, terminology (US or UK), and unique stitches
  - General pattern notes
  - Copyright or permission notes.

- Next is the meat of the document, the pattern instructions.

- The next section includes assembly instructions, if there are any.

- Detailed photos are inserted either throughout the document or placed in the back of the document.

- Before or throughout the pattern section are the helpful tips and suggestions, as it guides readers to better understand how to follow your instructions.
- Crochet techniques and tutorials are sometimes added at the beginning or end of the document.
- Author information is also added either at the beginning or end of the document.

Content Layout

Difficulty Skill Level

Noting a suggested difficulty level is subjective. The skill level honestly depends on the crocheter's personal knowledge and skill set. A novice and a beginner level crocheter could mean the same thing. But what about the difficulty level between an experienced beginner and an intermediate level crocheter?

It's more helpful to include what techniques and unique stitches are used in the pattern than to include a recommended skill level. This gives the crocheter an idea of what she needs to know before starting the pattern. For example, an advanced beginner crocheter may only know how to work in single and double crochets, do basic color changes, and back and front loops. If the pattern calls for special stitches like a picot crochet or a French knot, an experienced beginner may not be familiar with these techniques.

Suggesting your pattern at a beginner to experienced beginner skill level range increases people's likelihood of buying your pattern. It can be daunting for the potential buyer to see the suggestion level at an intermediate to advanced skill level range. Crocheters want to feel like they are buying something they can follow well enough to get a result similar to your finished object.

Experienced crocheters won't have to buy your pattern if they can "eyeball" your design. Even if you believe the pattern leans towards the intermediate skill level range, then rate your pattern at an experienced beginner's level.

If you want more sales, it's important to focus on the average crocheters than the few highly skilled crocheters. Rating a skill level is only a suggestion. Readers can judge for themselves what their skill level is by looking at the photos.

Materials and Supplies

The materials and supplies section is nice to have. However, many crocheters gloss over this section, as most crocheters already have a supply kit of scissors, tapestry needles, and stitch markers. It's optional to mention frequently used supplies in your document, as these are standard supplies needed in crochet crafting. But you never know if your pattern will be the first one someone attempts!

Some materials are essential to mention, such as safety eyes, the type and color of the yarn, and stuffing, as these impact how the finished object will turn out. For the eyes, mention the size you used for your finished item. Crocheters need to know what size to buy. You can make suggestions on how different size eyes can impact the look of an amigurumi as well. The larger the bead size, the more "bright-eyed" the amigurumi will look.

Another noteworthy mention is the yarn. Customers usually want to know the colors, brand, and type of yarn used so they can decide what to buy. The goal for the crochet buyer is to replicate your work. With so many different shades and hues of color yarns, it's good for customers to know where they can buy the same color yarn as the one shown in the pattern photo. The same goes with other supplies, such as the poly fiber stuffing and any craft wire. It's helpful to mention what materials to buy, especially if buyers are new to amigurumi. They may know how to crochet, but they might not be familiar with amigurumi. Provide lots of information and offer advice on the different materials, such as jewelry wire, pipe cleaner, foam hair curlers, cotton swabs, etc.

Measurement, Hook Size, Gauge

Including the dimensions of the finished object can be helpful so that the customer has an idea of how big their project will be. Of course the dimensions may vary slightly for each crocheter depending on the yarn used, hook size, tension, and the amount of stuffing used. Some crocheters simply estimate the finished object size based on the photos in your pattern. Most people don't grab a ruler and check the actual dimensions before purchasing the pattern. Make sure to be clear about the units of measure you used when providing dimensions, so that customers from any location know whether or not to convert to their standard units of measure – a 10 cm result might lead to disappointment if someone was assuming it was 10 inches!

It's more helpful for buyers if the finished product is photographed next to an everyday object, like a pencil or mug, for comparison. It gives the customer a better idea of height perception than the number noted in the posting and document. You can also include measurements of the different pieces and the final measurement of the finished work. For example, if you're making a llama with a sombrero, you can include separate measurements for the hat and the llama.

Suggested hook sizes and yarn gauges are informational only, particularly when making amigurumi. People usually use the crochet hook size they're comfortable with, or the size recommended on the yarn label. For example, if you're working with chenille yarn, the hook size tends to be bigger than cotton or acrylic yarn. Some crocheters also purposely use a hook size that is smaller than what is recommended in order to tighten the stitches and reduce the gaps between stitches.

Gauge doesn't matter too much in amigurumi. The gauge measures how loose or tight your work is, which determines the size of your work. For amigurumi, you want to crochet tight stitches to avoid holes in your work. You also don't want the stuffing to show through your amigurumi. Measuring the gauge is more relevant for garments, clothing, or accessories that must fit according to the body size, but not necessarily for amigurumi.

The gauge can help determine yardage/meterage, or how much yarn is used. Knowing the yardage helps determine how much yarn to buy. We all know how nerve-racking it is to play yarn chicken! If you don't want to list the gauge, it's nice to let your customers know how much yarn is needed.

Yarn and Recommended Hook Size Chart

NUMBER SYMBOL	1	2	3	4	5	6
CATEGORY NAME	Super fine	Fine	Light	Medium	Heavy	Very heavy
UK YARN TYPE	3 ply	4 ply	Double knitting (DK)	Aran	Chunky	Super chunky
US YARN TYPE	Fingering	Sport	Light worsted	Worsted	Bulky	Extra Bulky
UK HOOK SIZE #	13 - 9	9 - 7	7 - 5	5 - 3	3 - 00	00 - ⋯
US HOOK SIZE Letter (#)	B(1) to E(4)	E(4) to 7	7 to (I)9	I(9) to K(10½)	K(10½) to M(13)	M(13) and larger
HOOK IN METRIC SIZE (mm)	2.25 to 3.5	3.5 to 4.5	4.5 to 5.5	5.5 to 6.5	6.5 to 9	9 and larger

Abbreviations, Terminology, Unique Stitches, and General Pattern Notes

This section is one of the more informative elements to include. The standard terms and abbreviation section helps crocheters determine how to read your pattern before they begin. Even though it may be most common to use US terms these days, it's always good to note if your pattern is in US or UK terminology.

Consider including tutorial instructions for unique stitches. This way, crocheters can quickly find instructions for stitches they're unfamiliar with, or if you have a non-standard way of doing a stitch which your pattern depends on. Unique stitches can be any stitch that's not one of the following basic stitches: magic ring, chain, slip stitch, single and double crochet, back and front loop only. More complicated stitches might be the moss stitch, shell stitch, picot, or French knot.

If you include a tutorial for specialty stitches, or any stitch, make sure to mention this in your post when selling. Data shows that 93% of shoppers are more likely to purchase a product based on convenience. If the potential customer loves your design but is not familiar with how to create a French knot, they may be hesitant to purchase your pattern. The crocheter will be required to search online for instructions on how to crochet a French knot. But if you market your patterns with descriptive instructions, photos, visual aids, or even videos, buyers won't feel so intimidated. You want to reassure the customer that your knowledge and skills are transferable to them. As a pattern writer, you want your work to be repeatable and easy enough to replicate. The more information you include in your document, the more likely potential customers will feel good about buying your patterns.

General pattern notes are also helpful to include, especially when designers have their own style of writing patterns. This section helps the crocheter understand your pattern better. The following are some commonly used pattern notes:

- Work in a continuous spiral.

- Turning chains do not count as stitches.

- Instructions in parenthesis ( ) or brackets [ ] should be worked in the same stitch.

Copyrights and Permission Notes

You may have noticed there are no strict guidelines for how to write a pattern. It's up to the designer what to include in the pattern, including the copyrights and permission notes section. This section is optional, but it lets buyers know to respect the designer's work. You often see the following verbiage:

- The pattern is for personal use only.

- Do not distribute, reproduce, share, or sell this pattern or parts of this pattern.

- You may sell finished items but in limited quantities.

- Wholesale is not allowed.

- Please credit the designer.

Some customers tend to ignore this, especially when making finished items. Many crocheters make finished items for their friends and families, or sell hundreds of finished items at craft fairs. There are many designers who don't mind at all and actually appreciate the exposure. However, there are always a few designers sensitive to having crocheters turn their creations into a cottage industry. What designers are generally most concerned with are customers distributing their patterns without permission.

Designers include this section mainly to protect their written work. Designers don't want other designers passing it off as their own creation. It takes time to design something, crochet (and frog!) the work, write out the pattern, take photos, and then market the pattern. There's a lot of work that goes into producing a pattern. (That's one of the reasons why you bought this book.) Devaluing or stealing someone else's hard work isn't appreciated. This is the designer's way to explicitly but kindly ask customers to please respect their work and wishes.

Assembly

The assembly instructions are mentioned after the main body of the document. Instructions on assembling the product can be helpful, especially if many separate pieces need to be sewn together. Assembling parts is relatively intuitive, but suggesting which parts to be attached first, and so on, can be helpful to those who are new to the amigurumi world. For example, if your pattern is for a doll, the assembly order of when to attach the arms to the main body or when to attach the hair piece to the head may not matter much, but it may be a helpful reminder to indicate that the hair piece should be attached to the head before sewing the hat on.

This section also documents the last finishing touches, such as any embroidery add-ons or accessories. Taking the time to explain these add-ons and extra details is sometimes much more important than the instructions on how to attach the limbs. For example, you don't want the crocheter to forget to embroider facial features before closing the head of the doll.

Most pattern writers also include a "Job well done! You're finished!" commentary. The attaboy comment gives the crocheter a sense of accomplishment for completing the project and successfully following your pattern. It's a nice touch to include words of encouragement to your customer. It's also a helpful way to indicate that there are no more steps to follow, no more details, accents, or finishing touches.

2. PATTERN INSTRUCTIONS

The detailed crochet instructions is the star in your pattern. This section is the make-it-or-break-it section in your product. How good your pattern is, or isn't, will be the reason why you will get repeat business or not. Make sure to write clearly. The reader should be able to follow your instructions to ensure their finished work resembles yours, as shown in the photos. If the crocheter can easily replicate your amigurumi design, you'll probably gain a new repeat customer!

The format is written as a list of numbered instructions. It's easier to read a set of instructions step by step and line by line, where the next round starts a new line. It's different from writing a novel in one big paragraph; it's more like writing and reading a recipe.

There's no right or wrong way to write instructions but be consistent with your writing style throughout the pattern, and follow your abbreviations and pattern notes. For example, you can either write "2 sc in each st" or "inc", as it means the same thing. Another example is either using asterisks *..*, brackets [..], or parenthesis (..) when repeating in a row or round. For example, *Crochet *2 sc in each st*, repeat * (12)* or *[inc] x 6 (12)*. Both versions ultimately mean the same thing and will equate to a total of 12 stitches by the end. Whatever writing style you choose, it's best to stick to one.

Examples of Pattern Writing Styles

inc in all 6 st. [12]	[inc] x 6. (12)
6 inc. (12)	[inc] repeat 6 times. (12)
2 sc in each st. (12)	2 sc in next st, repeat around. (12)
2 sc in each st., repeat *. (12)	[inc] repeat to end. (12 sts)

Don't forget to include the stitch counts at the end of each round or row, and always check your stitch counts, multiples, and math. Crocheters who have crocheted enough amigurumi may be savvy enough to figure out and overlook a few math mistakes. But crocheters who are inexperienced with amigurumi will follow your pattern instructions down to the T. So having your math correct is very important. It's frustrating for crocheters to frog or unravel rows of hard work when they discover their stitch counts need to be corrected, not because it's their mistake, but the mistake in the pattern.

Also, break out the pattern sections in logical order. Have crocheters crochet the pieces in the order that makes the most sense. For example, if you're designing an animal, you might want to start by documenting the main body. Start with the legs, then the body, and then continue to the head. Afterward, you should document the separate body parts: the arms, ears, nose, and tail. The last step is to document the clothes and other accessories.

Some patterns mention the smaller pieces first, such as the body parts, since they're faster and easier to crochet. Sometimes, it's better to get the easy ones out of the way first. Make sure instructions for separate pieces are laid out consecutively, not scattered throughout the document. It gives the reader a clear idea of what's constructed. For example, if the pattern you're writing calls for 4 legs, 2 ears, 1 snout, and 1 tail, it's best to keep these instructions together.

Sometimes, the pattern can call for a break or pause from finishing a piece, particularly continuing with a one-piece such as a doll's main body. If the pattern is interrupted, explain why and when it will continue. For example, a pause to the doll's torso might be required to join with another piece, or to create an extension piece to the main body.

Some pattern pieces may also need to be repeated multiple times. Make sure to note how many times a section of the pattern will need repeating. An example would be crocheting 2 ears and 4 legs when writing out an animal pattern.

"All progress takes place outside the comfort zone."
Michael John Bobak

---

3. THE ESSENTIALS

Helpful Tips

In addition to writing clear instructions, a good pattern writer also includes helpful tips and tricks. The main part of a pattern is the written steps. However, written steps aren't always enough to fully understand how to create one's work. The more information you can provide to the crocheter on how to make your creation, the better. Anything you think needs further explaining or that will make your customer's crochet experience more pleasant can be a helpful tip. Tips can...

✦ Help explain crochet techniques.

✦ Clarify complicated color changes.

✦ Be instructional photos.

✦ Be additional information on the materials used.

✦ Be shortcuts for a crochet method.

✦ Provide explanations for complex steps.

Understanding crochet instructions can sometimes be frustrating for the average crocheter, especially those new to amigurumi. This is why it's helpful to include tips in your pattern. Tips can be noted anywhere in the document to help clarify any confusion. If you're unsure which part of the pattern needs more explanation, ask pattern testers for suggestions.

Sometimes, more words can lead to confusion, so keep your explanations clear and concise. As the pattern writer, you may understand your own written steps, but others may not. Have pattern testers read through your entire document to see if the pattern is clear enough. Photos accompanied by descriptive explanations can also go a very long way. Images can be more effective than words, especially if you need help explaining how a step should be carried out. During the crocheting and writing process, remember to stop and take photos. Be mindful of where to take certain breaks from crocheting so you can take helpful photos along the way.

Most crocheters like having informational details, but photos aren't practical when printing many pages. As a consideration, you can place helpful tips and photos at the end of the document. This way, it doesn't get in the way of cluttering the content flow of the actual crocheting instructions, and it also avoids unnecessary printing. Placing photos toward the end of the document also makes it easier for you to edit the document. You won't have to spend so much time reformatting photo layouts.

If you're putting tips and photos at the back of the document, say so at the beginning of the pattern. Say it's for the environment — crocheters might want to save ink and paper if the pattern is printed. Placing helpful tips and photos toward the end of the document might be a slight inconvenience for some customers, but they'll understand why if you state your reasons upfront.

Graphic Design

Making your pattern pages look awesome honestly shouldn't matter, but nowadays, it does make a difference to the buyer. Reading text on a white page may be seen as plain and boring. Adding pizzazz to the pages makes customers feel they're getting their money's worth because of the even more added details to the document, although it's not related to crochet making. Overall, it makes the final product of what you're selling professional looking.

Take, for example, the art of gift wrapping and the gift itself. When you give someone a present, part of the traditional gifting process includes wrapping. Of course, it's the gift inside all that colorful tissue paper or underneath that fancy bow and wrapping paper that counts. The gift is what matters, not the frills of tissue paper galore. But that extra love and attention to presentation does get noticed. The same goes for adding graphic designs to your pattern.

There are many free document or slide templates available online. Pick a themed template related to the finished object or that fits your personal brand and copy and paste your document and photos onto the template. You can also work directly onto the template, but it's easier to work from a simple, blank document first. Remember, your primary focus of what you're selling is the content of what's written in the document, not the page design. When choosing your page designs, refrain from drowning the customer with too much color or cute graphics. The focus needs to be on the pattern, not the borders, graphics, and fonts. Don't spend too much time working on template design. It's the pattern and information on the page that counts.

Pattern writers usually do a little something to make their pattern documents look more attractive, especially for marketing and social media purposes. It's a way for potential buyers to judge a book by its cover quickly. Detailed backgrounds or image-heavy templates can however make it hard for people who print patterns. Just as you need to approach the inclusion of photos with caution so that your patterns are easily printable, so too should you approach template design. Unnecessary graphics are a waste of ink, and many crocheters know that a pretty template doesn't add value to the pattern. You can still make your document look professional by adding minimal aesthetic touches, such as adding small icons to the page numbers, formatting font styles and sizes, and picking professional, easy-to-read fonts such as san serif fonts, should you choose not to use a decorative template.

"Intelligence without ambition is a bird without wings." Salvador Dali

---

4. PIGGYBACK OFF YOURSELF

Make Use of Your Other Income Streams

If you have customers buying your patterns, streamline your entrepreneurial efforts by sending them to your other businesses, social media content, or website. It's a seamless strategy to lure them to your blog or vlog. Customers appreciate having additional, related information provided to them. It's all about convenience for them.

If you want to share a lot of information with your buyers and fellow crocheters, it might not be practical to do it in one document. For example, a pattern tutorial or a CAL video is more helpful than just words and pictures on paper. You can share helpful tips in other places besides your pattern. Yes, tips and instructions are great. Refreshing one's memory on crochet techniques is also great. Why not direct your customers to your website or YouTube channel?

This is an opportunity to leverage your other crochet content. It's a one-stop shop and a great convenience for customers when they can read your pattern and watch how to complete specific steps without having to hunt for exactly what you mean. Include links directly to your video content in your pattern so customers know exactly where to get additional help. It gets you more visibility on your other content and the customer gets additional help without having to email you or enquire on forums.

"If you think you are too small to make a difference, try sleeping with a mosquito." Dalai Lama

---

Give Yourself a Shout Out

The short-sighted vision of writing and selling patterns is to crank out as many patterns as possible — as long as you have the drive, passion, and creativity. But it's important to think of the big picture as well. Think like a CEO and consider what that long-term vision should be. Your intent should not be just about producing patterns, but drawing in loyal, returning customers.

One way to do this is to introduce yourself in your pattern. The introduction doesn't have to be some lengthy autobiography but something sweet and short, along with providing your email address. This way, you've bridged the gap with the customer — from being a stranger to someone they can connect with at some level. It's important to also include a narrative about yourself on your e-commerce and social media platforms, but with the pattern in hand, the customer will always be reminded who the designer is — YOU.

If you've made a quality pattern with clear instructions, chances are your customers will remember you and be more inclined to give your other work a chance. A first-time buyer may not know it yet, but once they see your pattern, they might put you on a pedestal. Why? Because they're happy with their purchase, they like what they see, and they admire your work. They're pretty impressed by you!

Use this to your advantage and leverage your likeability by sharing with the customers more about yourself. As a result of a perceived connection between you and your customers, they may be more inclined to buy more of your patterns because they want to support you. Data shows that engaged customers help bring in 51% more revenue and sales than customers who aren't engaged with your brand and products.

Continue to leverage this connection by mentioning your business accounts for Instagram, Facebook, and other social media platforms on your pattern. This way, customers can continue to follow your work. The more you engage with your customers, the stronger the loyalty and relationship you'll have with them, as they become regular customers. Plus, they'll be more interested in you and your work when you share updates about what you're doing.

"You don't have to see the whole staircase, just take the first step."
Martin Luther King, Jr.

Praises, Pretty Please!

You are in control of the pattern you write. There's no final authority on what's the right or wrong way to write a pattern or what to include in a pattern. After you ensure a quality, clear pattern, use that document to sell YOU. Make everything in your document help sell more of your patterns and attract more customers. Have the customer do the work for you by bringing in more customers. If you mention your social media accounts in your pattern, ask them to tag you on their accounts when they finish their work.

Many crocheters love to share their finished work with their followers. They're proud of what they've accomplished! So why not piggyback on your customers? What's even better is that they have admirers, too. And the chances are, those admirers will come to purchase your patterns. If you're tagged, you can follow that posting thread and directly respond to comments. This way, the "student" (customer) feels acknowledged by the "master" (you), and their followers now have access to you as well. Marketing data shows that 64% of customers who feel valued are more likely to buy based on positive experiences over price. Here's an example of a shout out to add to your pattern:

✦ I'd love to see your work! Please share a photo with me on Instagram by hashtagging #XYZ and tagging me @XYZ.

One of the key strategies to success is also getting reviews from customers. Remember to ask customers to write a review on your e-commerce site. Explicitly mention this in your pattern. It doesn't hurt to ask, and you will probably get a few more reviews than if you didn't ask at all. Having as many reviews as possible is essential to growing your business.

When potential buyers are wavering on whether to buy your pattern, seeing the number of reviews may help convince them. When the pattern has many reviews, it reassures potential customers that it's okay to buy the pattern. It also makes them feel good about themselves, as this is called choice-supportive bias. They perceive they made the right choice in purchasing your pattern because others have also done so with satisfaction.

Secondly, if there are two patterns a potential buyer has to choose from — your pattern versus a competitor's — the deciding factors will likely boil down to which design looks better and how many reviews there are. While perceptions of "better" design are totally subjective when the pattern details cannot be read, how many reviews and the quality of them is more objective. A potential buyer is more likely to choose the the pattern with more (good) reviews. In terms of marketing, this is a simple numbers game. If there's a pattern with 0 reviews versus another pattern with 10 reviews, people will gravitate towards buying the pattern with 10 reviews. Which pattern would you buy if there's a pattern with 30 reviews versus another with 200?

Don't get caught up in fear of possible poor reviews. Try not to fear the worst and ignore the what-ifs in your head. If you're confident in the quality of your designs and how well-written your patterns are, you shouldn't be getting negative reviews. Also, a few bad reviews won't hurt your reputation, some people just like to complain and there is nothing you can do about them anyway.

If you happen to get 1 or 2-star reviews, potential customers will read the review to better understand why the poor rating.

In many cases, poor ratings aren't even related to the pattern itself. Some reviewers give poor ratings because English is not their first language, there weren't enough instructional photos to their personal liking, or they had technical difficulties downloading the pattern. Should you happen to receive a legitimate poor review, accept constructive criticism, and edit your pattern if needed.

In truth, not many people want to publicly be a bad guy and bash the pattern and the designer when most reviews are positive. This is also a choice-supportive bias. If most people give 4 or 5-star reviews, chances are others will agree. It's human nature for people to follow other people's actions and behaviors.

If a customer is frustrated and confused with your pattern, they will most likely reach out to you before finishing the project. When that happens, help the customer as best you can. A response from you will make the customer feel more at ease and help avoid a negative review. In this situation, however, be open-minded to see if your pattern needs updating. More than likely, the crocheter is a novice in amigurumi crocheting and just needed some friendly tutoring.

"If you want something you have never had, you must be willing to do something you have never done." Thomas Jefferson

---

5. WHAT'S IN A NAME

If you haven't come up with a crochet business name yet, it's time you create one, especially before you begin selling your pattern. It's important to give your brand an identity so people know who you are. Your crochet name can be whatever you want, but keep in mind how it might affect your business. Make sure to give some thought to your business name. Your business name will inform the identity, personality, and individuality of your business. It's how followers and customers see you.

If you want to increase sales, try to keep your business and social media names consistent. This way, people can trust they're one and the same. You want potential customers to easily reference who you are between your selling and social media platforms. More importantly, create a name that's simple and memorable so potential customers can search for your brand. Your name can be personal, or cute and catchy, but you may also want to include a keyword that's relevant to what you're marketing — words like crochet, toys, or amigurumi. Also avoid creating a long name or one with an underscore, hyphen, or special characters. It's easy for people to mistype or misspell the name if it's complicated and difficult to remember.

Don't restrict yourself by adding specific details or a focal point to your name. For example, if you're a New Yorker and you love all things New York, you may want to add NY to your name, but it could unintentionally limit your customer base. Customers from outside of the US may associate your brand with American-focused designs or think that you have nothing for someone who hasn't been to New York. Also, let's say you design amigurumi lovey blankets, and you want to somehow incorporate this in your business name. But what happens if you branch into other amigurumi designs later on?

Maybe you discover down the road that your name's been trademarked by someone else, the website domain is already used, or the name you chose no longer suits your branding. Whatever the reason may be, should you decide to change your name, make sure not to delete or remove your account, but simply change it. Once the name is removed, some platforms, such as Ravelry, permanently retire the name and the name can no longer be used by you or anyone else. You can deactivate your account or change your settings to private on some platforms, like Pinterest.

Make sure to let your followers know you're changing your name before you do it, so they're not confused. Keep in mind that your previously tagged posts and mentions may no longer work and remember to update any links or buttons or already published pattern files that include your former business name.

6. TRANSLATE YOUR WORK

It's probably not something you want to tackle at the moment, but you might want to consider translating your patterns at some point. Crochet is a hobby everyone enjoys, so why not take advantage of maximizing your sales in a global market? Making your designs available in multiple languages and expanding your brand reach is an easy way to attract new customers.

Crochet symbols allow you to universally translate your designs, but they're not as widely used in amigurumi patterns. Online translation programs like Google Translate and Grammarly can translate your written designs, but they're not always accurate, especially with technical terms and slang. You can find crocheters on Facebook interest groups who can help translate your work. Some may translate your work for free, while others will do it for a commission or royalty.

Some crocheters translate patterns as a side hustle, or they may already have a crochet business of their own. It's up to you how you want to run your business but consider having your translated patterns on someone else's site. Your crochet colleague from another country may already have a string of followers, and she may already have a thriving business. If you let your colleague host your translated pattern on her site, she might spend time promoting it. You might make less profit on that particular pattern, but you may have more sales in the end — your pattern and brand can just tag along for the ride!

Crochet Translation Reference

Symbol	US Abbr.	Spanish	French	Italian
⬯	ch	cadeneta (cad)	maille enl´air (ml)	punto catenella
●	sl st	punto enano (pe)	maille coulee	maglia bassissima
†	sc	punto bajo (pb)	maille serrée	maglia bassa (m. bassa)
⊤	hdc	punto alto (pa)	demi-bride (demi-br)	mezza maglia alta
⟊	dc	bride (br)	punto alto doble (pad)	maglia alta (m. alta)
⟊	tr	punto alto triple (pat)	double bride (d-br)	maglia altissima

CHAPTER 5

I IS FOR INVITING

"There are only two days in the year that nothing can be done. One is called Yesterday and the other is called Tomorrow. Today is the right day to love, believe, do and mostly live." Dalai Lama

1. A PICTURE IS WORTH A GAZILLION WORDS

You've heard the saying, "A picture is worth a thousand words." This is absolutely true!

Having quality photos is one of your top priorities when selling patterns. The first thing any potential customer sees is photos of your crochet work. Potential customers have no idea if your patterns are well-written or not. It all comes down to what they can see in the finished item.

Vision takes up 50% of our brain power, more than any other sense or ability. It takes 1/10th of a second to have the brain instantly react to visuals rather than reading text. Therefore, it's not just about taking photos, but taking good, compelling ones. If you're presenting poor quality photos to the world — blurry, uncentered, too dark, too busy — potential customers assume the same goes for your patterns.

The mind translates *bad photos* = *bad patterns*. Your photos are the first impression people have of your patterns. It may not be a direct reflection of your patterns, but an association with the quality of your work. In this day in age, everything is dependent upon social media and perception. Potential customers can only judge and go by photos at this point. To invest in your patterns, they must first like what they see. Seeing is believing, and if potential buyers see unflattering photos, what makes them believe your patterns are any different? To captivate an audience and bring in those sales, you've got to make your photos count in the fleeting moment you have their attention!

Home is Where the Heart Is

Even if you don't know the first thing about photography, there are a few simple housekeeping rules everyone should know when taking good photos. Take the word housekeeping figuratively and literally. Imagine guests coming over to your house. What do most people do in preparation for having guests over? The first things that come to mind are tidying up the house and removing all sight of mess and clutter. Next, open the curtains and blinds to allow natural light in. Guests expect the house to be clean when they arrive. What guest likes seeing dirty dishes or toys all over the floor? What guest wants to be greeted in a dark and dreary house? As a proper hostess, you change out of your pajamas and put on proper attire. You may also offer up some light refreshments for your guests.

Just as you would greet a guest at your home — a warm and welcoming place — this is how one should consider taking quality photos. A beautiful, inviting home does not mean a fancy mansion with a crystal chandelier hanging over the grand entrance hall — home is where the heart is. It's not about the camera you use; it's about how you take photos from the heart. A good picture is one that you won't forget. This is what you should aim for when taking photos of your crochet work. Make memories stick. Touch the minds and hearts of potential customers to encourage them to buy your pattern.

Photography Crash Course

Natural Light

Rule #1 in photography is utilizing natural light. You can buy equipment lighting or use your camera flash for indoor photography. You can also take photos at times of day when there's good lighting. Whether you take photos outdoors or indoors near a large window, avoid anything that will cast shadows over your work. Many photo editing apps can help make your photos look more professional if the lighting isn't perfect or if there are noticeable dark shadows in the shot.

Backdrop

Adding a backdrop or background is also important when taking photos. Just like using a graphic design template for your written pattern, having a backdrop makes the visuals more exciting and personal. It's an effective way to increase visual stimulation. Immediately grabbing the customer's attention is what you're hoping to achieve, but make sure the background is manageable. The background is to help accentuate what you're selling, not to divert attention from it. Graphic design and photo editing software apps have background features to help improve your photos.

Artist: oche pots

Props

Like the backdrop, adding props to the photoshoot helps elevate your crochet work. Props should lighten the mood and make the customer feel at ease. To avoid clutter, carefully arrange objects in the shot. Some objects fit together better than others. Selected props should complement your craftsmanship, not distract from it.

Depending on your finished work, commonly used props can be flowers, books, toys, or matching accessories that bring value to your amigurumi object. Be intentional with prop choices and see how props relate to the main subject. The right props can help people intuitively understand what you're selling. For example, if you're selling an amigurumi that's winter holiday themed, consider placing ornaments, fake snow, or other similar holiday themed trinkets in the shot. If you're selling an amigurumi design that is Back-to-School themed, use school related objects like a pencil, chalkboard, or ABC blocks.

Adding props in the background can be used for aesthetic reasons. Props can also serve a functional purpose, like comparing heights. Placing a common object next to your amigurumi gives height perspective. You can show the size of your finished work by placing something familiar next to it, like a teacup or book.

Artist: Curious Papaya, Blue Rabbit Toys

Angles

Taking photos from different angles can be very helpful for potential buyers, as it offers different looks and perspectives for the same object. Top and side view angles help show off details that would not be visible if photos were taken from the front. Close-up photos can be helpful, too, especially if your design has small details and embellishments. Just make sure your crochet skills are good; you want to avoid exposing any flaws, such as inconsistency or gaps in your stitches. Customers may like your design, but poor craftsmanship can turn people away. Don't give people the opportunity to nitpick.

Flat lay has also been a popular trend for taking crochet photos. The finished object is laid on a flat surface, such as a poster or bed. The photo is then taken directly from above, similar to a bird's eye or aerial view. The flat lay shots usually look better because it shows more surface area than if taken upright. However, taking photos from above can cast a shadow. To prevent this, ensure you're far enough from your objects with some shade directly above you to block any direct sunlight.

Artist: Airali Design

2. THE DEVIL IS IN THE DETAILS

When in Doubt, Leave It Out

Investing in props can get quite expensive. Or maybe you're not ready to give up your yarn allowance yet. Another method for effective photo-taking is to keep things simple. If you have decent lighting, taking photos of your finished work with a white background can be sufficient for taking quality photos. It's not necessary to have all the frills. The focus is to let your artwork speak for itself. You can never go wrong with the minimalist look. Sometimes, less is more.

Rather than using physical props, you can use text to help draw attention to your photos. A simple photo can still speak volumes and capture the audience's heart by adding text to the photo. People appreciate words of affirmation and inspirational quotes. Words can be just as compelling as visuals. The brain processes and reacts slower to things that have to be read, rather than taking in a text-free visual, but with nothing else in the background, the emphasis is on the finished object.

When potential buyers read empowering words on the screen and then see your finished work next to it, the text and the object now have a connection. There's an association created between your work and the message. For example, when crocheters read a mother-and-child quote that emotionally moves them overlaid with your amigurumi lovey security blanket, they are more likely to think of your item in the same way as the quote. Potential buyers are now likely to think of your pattern as a great baby shower or grandchild's gift. Not all text and visual connections have to be deeply emotional, you can also use common associations to your advantage. A text saying "Trick or Treat, Smell My Feet" is easily associated with playful Halloween amigurumi. Keep it simple and let words be your props.

Cameos

One reason for adding backdrops and props to photos is to bring additional context to the main subject in the photo. Rather than using the common household, everyday objects such as plants and toys for your props, or objects you purchase at the arts and crafts store, use your other finished works as props to increase brand awareness.

Once you have more patterns, you can showcase your latest work with past products in the same photos. This strategy marries well with objects that are of similar designs or niches. Seeing like-props in the background amplifies the theme and subject matter. Also, new buyers may be more likely to purchase your other patterns when they see them styled with what they are looking at now. The same is also true of existing customers that missed out on a pattern, so make the most of this familiarity past customers already have with you.

Artist: Julia Ka Pattern

Pairings

When designing and writing your pattern, it's good practice to crochet the same pattern again. Your second attempt will always turn out better than your first. This is because of muscle memory and because you're no longer in that designing and writing mode but in the phase of reading and following a pattern. You can use this second finished object as a photo prop. Rather than repeating the pattern with the same colors, change it by altering the colors for your second finished item. Choose a new set of colors that pairs well with your first make. When you're ready to take photos, strategically position the two finished objects from different angles. Viewing identical objects in the same photo but in different angles and colors gives potential buyers a comparative view and a different perspective of the two objects.

Another strategy is to crochet the same pattern, but rather than using different colors, this time use a different yarn weight or type instead. The outcome between the two finished pieces will be the difference in scale and/or texture. The pairings of the same object in different yarns help customers see all the potential in your pattern.

Artist: Storyland Amis

Balance		An object that is not overpowered by another object. (Symmetrical, asymmetrical, equal, distribution of weight.)
Contrast (Variety)		Focuses on different elements, establishes hierarchy and organization.
Emphasis (Focal point)		Focuses on an object to make it stand out.
Harmony (Unity Comparison)		Combines similarities, emphasizes on relationship, focuses on cohesion.
Pattern (Repetition)		The repeating of shapes and other elements in an organized or random order.
Rhythm (Movement)		Following the path of an object. (Juxtaposition, eye movement, physical movement.)
Scale		The relative size of one object compared to another.

Disrupting the Norm

With so much visual overload from social media these days, some viewers have become desensitized to perfectly arranged, professional-looking photos. A good marketing tactic is to disrupt the status quo. Find ways to break the "as expected" mold while making photos compelling enough for viewers to get their attention. Mix things up and include photos that are more than just finished works.

Examples to include in postings can be showcasing instructional photos or projects that are still a work in progress. These different perspectives make your patterns and marketing stand out and might get a better reaction from your target audience. Scrolling through all the perfectly arranged props in photos can get boring. Viewers are so used to seeing completed works, it's refreshing to see different styles for a change.

Instruction photos can also help viewers understand the "big picture" when descriptive words fall short. But more importantly, many people are just visual learners. If videos are an option, include short clips in your online postings. For some people, videos are more helpful when learning something new than just still photos. Visual learners crave videos and photos because they capture attention better, help maintain focus, and are more easily retained in memory, far better than reading instructional text.

Offering helpful tips upfront or showing play-by-play photos intrigues potential customers, making them feel like they are going to get a lot for their pattern price. Also, engaging the audience is easier when a learning environment is involved. There's more context sharing than just the finished product of still photos. A journey process is shared.

Photos can also include excerpts from the written pattern you're selling. Potential buyers think they're getting a freebie from the pattern. With only part of the pattern revealed, they're left wanting more. It also allows them to decide for themselves if your pattern is well written or not. If they understand your writing style before they have to commit to a purchase, you'll have fewer situations of buyer's remorse or people needing advice after a purchase. You've proven to them your designs look good, and your writing is good before you took their money.

Photo marketing methods can help you better engage with potential customers. Visual teasers can prompt curiosity in potential customers and encourage them to start a crochet journey with your patterns.

3. SHOWER CONSUMERS WITH CUTENESS

The best kinds of photos are the ones that make a lasting impression. Memorable photos are the ones that captivate and play on one's emotions. Your photos need to convince potential customers that they want your patterns over other designers. Your patterns are the chosen ones. But how do you outshine your competitors? Potential customers don't know you and honestly have no reason to get to know you. Instead, it's your job to show them what you can offer them and why. And to do that, it's all about selling with emotions — their emotions. This is how you get to a buyer's heart and then purse strings.

Listen to Your Heart

When it comes to purchasing, customers can do all the research in the world by looking at prices and reading descriptions of products. Customers click that "buy now" button because of an emotional pull, that strong urge to buy a product decided by the heart. For many crocheters, rationale gets thrown out the window when it comes to buying yet *another* crochet pattern. It's a guilty pleasure that can't be helped! More often than not, consumers decide with their hearts instead of their heads. And crocheters rely on emotion to make decisions most of the time!

The Heart Wants What It Wants

Ask yourself, "How much yarn do you really need, and how many more patterns do you really have to buy?" Contrary to what your significant other or spouse believes, your answer probably is, "I can never have enough!" These are questions that crocheters and crochet sellers would rather not think about.

Psychology explains that human behavior is motivated by needs and desires. Needs come first, and needs are the basic requirements for survival, such as food, shelter, and safety. Desires, or wants, are secondary. However, there's often a conflicting balance between needs and wants, especially when wants are separated from emotional needs by a fine line. The mind of a crochet consumer can easily be convinced that "I *must* have this for my newborn!" Make buyers believe your patterns are no longer a want but a need. As the seller, it's important to leverage these emotions. Create photos that blend the psychological and emotional motivators of needs and wants. For example, commercials with babies, puppies, kittens, grandparents, and families are designed to make people feel sentimental, and customers can relate to that. This is the kind of brand imagery you want to market.

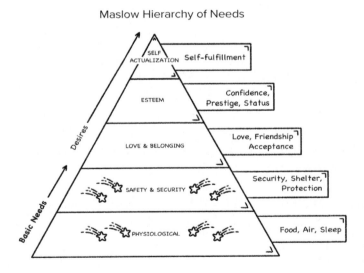

Maslow Hierarchy of Needs

Have your kids and pets be your models. Take photos of your son playing with the amigurumi dinosaur you designed. Take a picture of your dog napping with the amigurumi toy you made for him. These photos simulate the human bond between the buyer and their loved ones, all while showing your products integrated into the experience. As the seller, presenting the potential buyer with images that prompt feelings of happiness and scenes that they can identify with tells the buyer you're able to relate to their life, and they in turn are more likely to trust your products.

Some people may not feel comfortable showing their faces on camera. Instead, consider taking photos of a child's hand placed over the amigurumi toy. It displays the physical attribute, height and scale, and the emotional attribute of a loved one, without violating privacy. Have your photos capitalize on this level of human connection, intertwining wants and needs. If you can accomplish this, you'll have buyers lining up to your shop to buy your patterns.

"A river cuts through rock not because of its power, but because of its persistence." Jim Watkins

---

4. TURN INFINITY INTO AFFINITY

When you see or hear something enough times, the message starts to stick with you. People aren't tied to the product when it's out of sight and out of mind. But when the image becomes ingrained in one's mind, the brain begins to get used to seeing that same or similar image over and over. The brain is now telling the potential buyer this is something that is missing in one's life, and it's now something the buyer wants to purchase.

One of the annoying, but powerful, use of social media is getting the word out. It's also an effective platform that brings people's attention and awareness. So, when it comes to your marketing efforts, post the heck out of your photos! Your marketing efforts can be on Pinterest, Instagram, Facebook, or any other social media platform that helps get you access to potential customers. Post, repost, and recycle through as many photos as you can. Post photos of your new and old patterns as often as possible, ideally a few times a week and multiple times throughout the day.

When viewers see your posts enough times, there's a good chance they'll end up reacting to the photo and hopefully, buying the pattern. They can place the pattern in their shopping cart, pin it, like it, or share it. Whatever the outcome, your efforts were worth it if you got their attention. The idea of social media marketing can get tedious, but why miss out on this strategy when others are doing the same? That constant presence might just maneuver your pattern to the front of the checkout line. If you're occasionally posting, it's less effective than if you post on a regular, active basis. Keep posting and make this an ongoing ritual. You are more likely to draw in more potential customers with frequent appearances in their feeds than if you post irregularly.

In a way, this strategy can also be considered a "caving in" tactic. Some customers are reminded so often that they eventually submit to their temptations and purchase the product. A sale is a sale! It doesn't matter how you get that sale. There's a saying that goes, "If you throw enough spaghetti at the wall, one is bound to stick." Social media presence is an absolute must to help increase your sales.

It's essential to still be mindful of the quality of the photos you're producing. It's good to continue to post engaging and emotionally compelling photos. Though part of selling efforts is to post on a routine basis, you still want to be relatable and likable. Imagine those holiday movies that are shown on TV every year. Some movies can get tiresome, but some are just classics, and you don't mind watching that same heartfelt movie with the family time and time again.

Brand imagery is also essential to consider when you share photos on repeat. Strategically, it's beneficial for photos to look consistent with similar photo layout styles and storytelling styles. Just as people recognize your crochet work by looking at one photo after another, you want people to recognize who you are through your brand. That familiarity and likeness through brand recognition keep you connected with potential customers, but more so with repeated customers.

Is there ever a stopping point to this infinite loop of posting? The answer is no. When Coca-Cola stops marketing, you can too. If you want your business train to keep moving, it's up to you to keep the train from not stopping. For you to juggle and manage multiple social media platforms and take the time to create, design, and write patterns, all of this can wear anyone down.

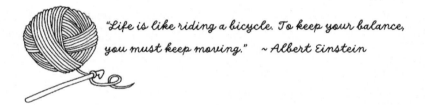

"Life is like riding a bicycle. To keep your balance, you must keep moving." ~ Albert Einstein

However, keep in mind that this isn't a rat race. You're in it for the long haul. That means to pace yourself and avoid burning the candle at both ends. You're in a hobby business that you love and want to enjoy years from now. Do what you can on your own time, as long as you start. You don't have to cross everything off the to-do list. The more you can accomplish, the more lucrative your business will be. But don't let the business overtake your life or ruin your love of crochet.

CHAPTER 6

N IS FOR NICHE

"The secret of getting ahead is getting started." Mark Twain

1. SQUIRREL!

When figuring out what patterns you want to design and market, finding a niche as early as possible is best. You want to focus on your strengths for your own sanity. You'll get burnt out if you're unfocused and scatter-brained with your business plans. You may feel overwhelmed, overthinking what designs you should be making. It's best to stick with what you know and what you're good at.

Why is it so important to pick a niche? Ultimately, it's about consumer preference and loyalty. Think back to the 80-20 rule in Chapter 1. Your goal in sales is to be efficient at marketing and rack up sales. The best way to generate those high numbers is from repeat customers and brand awareness. Think of Starbucks or Coca-Cola versus Pepsi. Avid coffee drinkers are not often daily tea drinkers. They also don't drink just any coffee, but usually a particular roast and brand. Take the classic example of Coca-Cola versus Pepsi. People who like soft drinks tend to be loyal only to Coca-Cola or Pepsi, not both.

Lastly, look at your own stash of yarn. You may have explored a few brands at first, but there are certain ones you keep going back to.

Consumers know what they like. On occasion, people can change their preferences. But for the most part, once they're comfortable with a particular product and brand, they're often loyal to the end. This is why it's so important to find your niche, and make the most of it.

You might be tempted to explore a few different areas or themes, but it's best to focus on one when you're first starting out. You want to make sure you can grow your sales and customer base before expanding your portfolio. Should you branch out into other niches, keep your curiosities to a minimum. You want to diversify your income streams, not your specialty.

Be forewarned that exploring and expanding into other categories will take time and resources away from your original focus. It's more efficient to focus on your repeat customers who are already familiar with your design style than grasping for new customers with different design preferences. To build a well-established business is to build a well-established, consistent customer base.

Starbucks expanded its business model in 2010 to include alcoholic beverages and the happy hour vibe, serving cocktails and appetizers. Obviously, they're known for selling coffee and selling the ambiance of the café experience. By 2017, Starbucks closed this chapter in their lives. It ultimately failed because everyone knows and recognizes the Starbucks brand as coffee. For the sake of your crochet branding, commit to the customers who already love you for who you are.

2. KNOW YOUR STRENGTHS

The easiest and quickest way to choose a niche is to crochet what you want to crochet and to make sure you're good at it. A niche can be any specialty if the style, purpose, or category is consistent. You're naturally more productive when you create works you want to design. Your passion maintains your interest through the hard bits and will keep your creative juices flowing. You want quality patterns, not just quantity of patterns. If you like what you're doing, it will feel less like work. You won't feel forced and you'll be more willing to persevere through designer's block until you are back in the rhythm of cranking out patterns as you can write them down! Do what you like and what you're good at, and eventually, things fall into place.

"The only reason for time is so that everything doesn't happen at once." Albert Einstein

---

Don't Rush the Process

Investing your time with only one or two patterns when you first start is important. You're bound to make some business and operations mistakes — and that's okay! You don't know what you don't know yet. Starting with just a couple of patterns gives you the breathing room to fix any issues that arise with your new business. If your early patterns don't meet your sales expectations, the first thing you're going to question or blame is your crochet skills and talents, and that's often not the case at all.

It's essential to see how your efforts play out from the beginning to the end. Take your first pattern through the entire development process and see how well it sells. It's harder to improve when you release a bunch of patterns all at once. With the focus on designing one pattern first, you can discover your mistakes early on and quickly learn and adapt from this. Not rushing to release patterns will also prevent those initial mistakes from appearing in other patterns shortly after the release of the first. When it comes to the next pattern, you will be more confident and comfortable with the process and better prepared for what your next moves are. You may be eager to start on the next pattern before the lifecycle has been completed on the first, but be patient with the process before moving on.

"Strive not to be a success, but rather to be of value." Albert Einstein

---

3. LISTEN TO WHAT THE MARKET HAS TO SAY

Even though it's easiest to focus on a niche you're passionate about, there are 3 criteria everyone needs to consider when starting a successful crochet design business. The third item is often ignored because it's not the path of least resistance and is something you only have limited control over. The 3 criteria are:

(1) Do what you like.

(2) Do what you're good at.

(3) Do something marketable.

Don't dwell too much on the first two criteria — those are easy. To make money from crochet, you need to understand what consumers want, and that comes down to marketing. What's not easy is to accept what the market is telling you. If you're in the crochet business to earn money, you must understand what consumers want, otherwise, you could give your patterns away for free. Do your market research: look at market trends, identify what the market needs are, and pinpoint what the market lacks.

This is one of the reasons why it's essential to start with just one pattern first. The business process is a learning curve —

you can learn how to run your business and you control your business. But you can't control the market. So, if you need to switch to a more marketable niche, it's easier to do it early on in your business. But remember, when you're working on your first pattern, you have to see it through to the end and assess the entirety of the process before deciding what's next. The market only tells you if your product works when you give it time in the marketplace.

It's Not Just the Looks That Matter

Finding a niche in amigurumi is often looking at the design of the artwork. When amigurumi designers think of the word niche, what comes to mind is designing styles specifically for doll patterns, animal patterns, gnome patterns, etc. A niche doesn't have to be about creating different looks; it can also be how products are made or what the product is.

Amigurumi is actually a niche within crochet; it's the hand making of toys. Other crochet niches can be corner-to-corner (C2C) crochet for blankets and pillows, appliques and silhouettes, or traditional crochet for garment wear. With so many ways to categorize crochet, there are also lots of ways to market and categorize amigurumi beyond just looks.

Think out of the box. A niche can be a twist in your marketing playbook. What can you do with amigurumi patterns other than creating different looks for toys? An example of a niche that is not focused on looks is creating patterns for pocket-sized amigurumi. Marketing "quick and easy" crochet ideas can be a niche. It serves a specific group of consumers who prefer to make small-sized toys or things that are quick to whip up.

If a crocheter mom wants to make 30 birthday favors for her child's party, what amigurumi should she be making? For this example, the market tells us there's a gap in the available patterns. The consumer parent is looking for an amigurumi pattern that's more convenient, not necessarily cuter.

Artists: Chai Coffee Crochet, Mikado Cute

4. MONEY OR FAME

Some crocheters may just want to enjoy the simple life of crochet, the occasional makings of their own design patterns, and the flexibility of designing whatever pattern they want without sticking to a niche path. Some are interested in designing and selling patterns, but many may find it challenging to stay disciplined, and to follow and cross off certain checkboxes to start, build, and sustain a pattern design business of their own.

It's okay if you want to earn passive income but you just don't feel like working so hard. There's always the potential to generate revenue, it's just usually dependent upon how much work is put in and how efficient you are with the work you put in. As mentioned in Chapter 1, it is important to acknowledge the difference between financial results and financial success.

The Silent Partner

Rather than building a complete empire on or of your own, why not have someone else sell the patterns for you? Why not consider freelancing or selling your pattern for royalty or commission under someone else's crochet business instead? By no means does this imply you threw in the towel too early, you quit, or that you were defeated. It's just another method of

selling your work. It may not be the typical passive income crocheters think about. However, the concept of making something once and having money rolling in is still there. You may
like the idea of being a designer and earning passive income,
but not necessarily everything else that goes with the business
side of it.

If you're thinking about selling your pattern to an existing
business, reach out to existing pattern writers, bloggers, magazines, or anyone with the infrastructure, operations, and sub-
scribers set up; and negotiate a business deal. The negotiation
and contract should include clear financial terms and rights
of ownership. Some established pattern designers who already
have their foot off the gas pedal may be open to your business
proposition! They're happy with the passive income they're
bringing in, and there's no need for them to hustle and grind
as much anymore.

Some may be willing to have a silent partner designing patterns
under their name. You may already be familiar with their work,
so the proposal to pass your work as theirs may not be so
far-fetched. There could be the question you may need to ask
yourself, though, of possibly forfeiting your work and recognition. This might not be an issue if your goal has been pursuing
your interest and making money, rather than fame.

"A group becomes a team when each member is sure enough of
himself and his contribution to praise the skills of others." Norman
Shidle

Two Heads Are Better Than One

Starting a crochet business doesn't necessarily mean you have
to start a business alone. There are a lot of moving parts to
starting and making a business succeed besides designing a pattern when that can be a challenge in itself. An option to consider when selling patterns is to partner with another designer

who's also starting out. Setting up a crochet pattern business doesn't have to be a one-person show. In fact, there are several crochet bloggers and online sellers that are actually a two-person act. Of course, there are logistics to determine who will be responsible for what, and maybe some butting of heads, but having someone that's equally invested in the business and able to split the workload may be the way to go.

It's intimidating to initiate the first step, but reach out to other beginner designers to enquire if they'd be interested in teaming up. You can make inquiries on social media or find new, interested designers on Ravelry or crafting sales platforms. Some crocheters go on Facebook groups asking to follow one another's Instagram. Here would be an opportunity to make your introduction and proposal.

CHAPTER 7

K IS FOR KINKS AND KICK-OFF

"If everyone is moving forward together, then success takes care of itself." Henry Ford

Once the writing part is done, it's time to find some pattern testers. Who are pattern testers, and why is it important to have them? These are volunteer crocheters who proofread and check your draft pattern before you officially publish your work. Proofreading patterns is much more than just reading through your document to check for grammatical errors. It involves someone thoroughly checking the overall understandability of the pattern. Ultimately, you will need another set of crocheter eyes to assess your work.

If you're having people pay for your pattern, ensure the document's quality, accuracy, and clarity are on point. Does the content flow make sense to the pattern reader? Are your instructions clear enough to follow? When they follow your pattern, will their finished work turn out the same as yours? Does the math check out? Which areas in the pattern need more explanation? These are some of the questions you hope to get answered by the pattern testers. You want honest, unbiased feedback before releasing your paid pattern.

What you want to avoid happening is releasing your pattern and then having paying customers discover these flaws. If that happens, this could detrimentally impact your future sales. You can receive poor reviews, which then turns future customers away. You definitely won't see these unhappy customers again when the goal was to turn them into repeat customers. Of course, you want to release your pattern as soon as possible to get those sales and work on the next pattern. Still, you want to ensure a quality pattern gets released before anything else.

"Even if you fall on your face, you're still moving forward."
Victor Kiam

---

1. SET EXPECTATIONS FOR PATTERN TESTERS

The best way to seek out pattern testers is through Ravelry or social media platforms. All you do is share a post of your finished work and ask crocheters if they'd be willing to test out a free pattern. Of course, many crocheters will be more than willing to help since you're giving away the pattern for free.

The number of testers you want is up to you. Since you're seeking volunteers, make sure you communicate your expectations before sending out your pattern to the testers. Give them a deadline for when they should finish their work and send you their edits. It's essential to give a strict deadline since you'll also need time to compile everyone's feedback and make your own final edits. It's at your discretion whether to accept their input or not. It's also good practice to collect email contacts. Communication via email keeps you more organized than the back-and-forth of social media direct messages. Plus, keeping a contact list allows you to communicate with testers to request their assistance in the future.

2. THE SECOND-BEST KEPT SECRET TO GROWING YOUR BUSINESS

Gathering pattern testers is truly one of the best kept secrets to building a pattern design business. So now that you're connected to a group of crocheters who are happy and willing to help test patterns, why not ask them for other favors?

When pattern testers complete their finished work, kindly ask them to take a photo of the amigurumi they made. It shows that your instructions are clear and intuitive enough for others. It also reveals if the pattern testers you chose are good crafters and good photographers. If the pattern tester is both a talented crocheter and photographer, see if they'd be interested in taking photos on your behalf. Of course, you should acknowledge and credit them if you include their work in your marketing.

Once your pattern is ready to be released or published, kindly ask your testers to post their finished work on their social media accounts and mention your business name. Leverage your new friendships and have them get the word out for you. Pattern testers are indeed a godsend! Take the time to thank them!

"Courage is like love; it must have hope for nourishment."
Napoleon Bonaparte

3. LOVING YOUR SECOND BORN AS MUCH AS YOUR FIRST BORN

Should you have more than enough test volunteers, don't write off the ones you decided not to use. Instead, kindly explain to them that you have enough pattern testers and would love to use them when your next pattern comes around. Ask for their email addresses so you can stay in touch and send them a coupon code for the pattern when it's for sale. This way, they won't feel disappointed for not being selected as a pattern tester. They might still be interested in your pattern, even if it's not for free.

See if this group is willing and open to helping you with another task instead. If they purchase your pattern with the coupon code, ask them to leave an honest review of the pattern as soon as possible. You want them to finish the project but for a different purpose. Hopefully, with a generous enough discount, these crocheters will be willing to leave an honest review for you.

Having early purchases and early reviews of a newly-released pattern right off the bat will help boost your sales. It shows that there's social proof when potential customers see other customers buying and liking your pattern. Why not start with a bang and get as many hits, likes, and reviews as possible for a new pattern? A powerful strategy to drive more sales is more reviews. This second set of volunteers-turned-early-customers will help you get sales going. Your early customers deserve as much thanks and appreciation as your testers.

CHAPTER 8

L IS FOR LAUNCH

"What is not started will never get finished."
Johann Wolfgang von Goethe

1. THE FINAL COUNTDOWN

The pattern is complete, the document has been converted into a PDF file, and it is now ready for release. Now you need to decide how to price your pattern and where to sell your digital pattern. Many e-commerce sites do digital selling. The most common crochet sites to sell patterns are Etsy, Ravelry, and Lovecraft. Though there's a learning curve on how to use each platform, start with one and eventually work your way to learn at least one more. Of course, the more marketplaces you sell, the more sales and money you make. Below are the pros and cons of each platform. It boils down to your preference for usability — from both the seller's and the customer's perspectives — and profitability.

Etsy

Etsy is the most popular, high-traffic site of the three mentioned platforms. Etsy is a publicly traded company; its commercials and marketing ads can be seen everywhere. Overall, Etsy's user interface is fairly easy and intuitive to set up an online shop. There are a lot of instructional videos the company provides on its site, along with its community boards and customer service team. There are other benefits Etsy provides that are outside of just wanting to sell your crochet items. These include tax and financial reports, sales tracking data, and marketing tools.

However, the two biggest drawbacks to Etsy are the hefty fees for sellers and the difficulty of downloading patterns for customers. Etsy has fees on top of fees that cut into the seller's profits. Your costs help sustain all those nice features Etsy has to offer. The second drawback is pattern downloads, which can be confusing for buyers. Crochet customers, especially those unfamiliar with Etsy, often end up contacting the seller, asking why they haven't received their pattern. Even after explaining how to download it on Etsy, the seller eventually just emails the pattern to the customer. As part of any shopping experience, transactions are supposed to be seamless. But Etsy doesn't make it easy to sell digital items. Some pattern sellers steer away from Etsy because of these headaches. If you sell on Etsy, be prepared to provide some customer technical support for things that are out of your control, and pay a hefty portion of your revenue.

Ravelry and Others

Ravelry is a marketplace specifically selling knitting, crochet, and other related fiber arts patterns. The Ravelry platform caters to not just crocheters, but all "yarnies" (or yarn hobbyists), whereas Etsy is a marketplace with a broader focus on handmade products. With Ravelry being a niche site better suited for crocheters, you know customers on Ravelry are on the hunt for patterns.

The best part about selling on Ravelry is that the seller fees are pretty reasonable, so you get to keep more money in your pocket when you make a sale. Profits are definitely higher compared to Etsy. The disadvantage, however, is its smaller customer base. So even if the percentage to pocket more money is higher, the sales volume may be more significant on Etsy than on Ravelry. But even that depends. Ravelry is a no-bells-and-whistles platform compared to its Goliath competitor. Because Etsy is a more extensive marketplace, your competition is more fierce. This means you need good marketing, search engine optimization (SEO), keyword searches, and photo skills.

With Ravelry being a no-frills site, maneuvering around the site has its challenges. It's not very intuitive to post and sell patterns from the seller's standpoint. From the buyer's standpoint, however, Ravelry makes it super easy for buyers to download patterns. Ravelry has done a great job with its file management system for downloading, storing, and organizing patterns. The digital file gets directly emailed to the buyer, along with having a library of stored patterns residing in Ravelry. It's easy to locate and find one's patterns when using Ravelry — an area Etsy clearly lacks.

Additionally, suppose you need to make corrections to your patterns. Maybe you wish to make changes to your already released patterns, and you want to let past customers know there's a revision. On Ravelry, you can notify past customers all at once to have them download the newest versions. Etsy doesn't have this feature.

Another commonly-used pattern site is LoveCrafts. LoveCrafts is a hybrid between Etsy and Ravelry, as it's a niche site that caters to artists and crafters, selling yarn, crafts, baking supplies, as well as digital patterns. The fees are low, so sellers can make a decent profit. The disadvantage with LoveCrafts is the lag time to receive funds compared to the other two competitors. The release of patterns can also be relatively slow, as it needs to go through an approval publishing process on the site.

Pricing

Figuring out what price to set can be intimidating for any first-time seller. If you've sold handmade products before, you probably started by underpricing them. You were probably worried that no one would come to your booth to buy anything. But as you became more confident with selling and you slowly fulfilled your immediate gratification needs, you re-examined how you priced your items. You considered the cost of materials, compensation for at least some of the hours put into making your items, and the price of other competitors. The same strategy can be applied when pricing your patterns.

Price your work according to what feels right to you but remember not to sell yourself short. For example, suppose your patterns are relatively common, where you might find similar designs for free. In that case, you may have to price your designs at a lower price. On the other hand, if your designs are more decorative than the common apples and pumpkin patterns, price them comparable to other designers in your niche. Finally, if you're feeling insecure about setting the same price as your competitors, start with a low price to get a few customers in the door, and then implement a higher price later on.

You also have the option of using coupon codes and promotional discounts. There's no right or wrong way to set prices; you can always change your prices. Don't worry about putting potential customers off if your price changes. If potential customers haven't bought your pattern yet, they're probably still undecided. If customers like your design, a slight price increase won't stop them from buying your work.

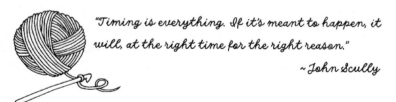

"Timing is everything. If it's meant to happen, it will, at the right time for the right reason."

~ John Scully

Luck or Timing

Your pattern is ready for release. You're hopeful your pattern will sell well, and you're ready to start on the next one. When making your debut, keep in mind that timing may affect your sales. Generally, the lowest sales month of the year is January, as many people have already made huge purchases in the prior months from the holidays.

Consider launching prior to seasonal trends, as events and special occasions are always cyclical and are routinely on people's minds. If you have a heart pattern, consider launching prior to Valentine's or Mother's Day. Likewise, if you have a Back-to-School themed pattern, launching in early summer may not result in very high sales, as consumers are not thinking of the classroom setting and homework during their time off from school. Same goes with Christmas patterns. The launching of nutcrackers and snowmen may be the last thing on a crocheter's mind during the spring or summer season.

Even though your launch timing may be off, it's still best to launch when you complete your pattern. People may hit the like button or save it in their carts. When the appropriate season comes around, send potential buyers a coupon. Sometimes it's not the pattern itself, but timing, that results in low sales. Lastly, the best time and biggest push to promote and launch your patterns is in the fall and early winter, as these are the highest purchase seasons for many consumer industries.

"You miss 100 percent of the shots you never take." Wayne Gretzky

2. T.E.A.M.: TOGETHER EVERYONE ACHIEVES MORE

There are a few things you should do before releasing your pattern and clicking that "publish" button. Crucial steps for success have been sprinkled throughout the book, but it's good to review some of these steps to ensure you're ready for launch day. Of course, the most critical step to get people to check out your pattern is spreading the word and bringing in as much traffic to your pattern site as possible.

That means sharing posts about your pattern on as many platforms as possible, and as frequently as possible. Circulate and cycle through your photos. Viewers will visit your pattern site if your visuals and storytelling are intriguing and captivating. Your job now is to repeat these steps consistently — not just for your newly released pattern, but for all patterns. But remember, you're not alone in this launch. Don't forget to bring your team with you.

With the followers you already have and the pattern testers and early customers you've gained, it's essential to tap into this network of yours and leverage them. Even if you just set up a Pinterest account yesterday or only have a handful of followers on your Instagram or Facebook, make do with what you have. Everyone starts from zero.

Going from a great idea to a money-generating pattern that sells like crazy is about taking your time, building trust, and most importantly, growing your team. Remember to have them post, share, and write reviews to support you. It takes a village to grow a successful pattern design business. Your success cannot be credited to you alone, but to the people who support you.

3. MATH IS EVERYWHERE

With the help and support of your team, your pattern and business will grow much faster than if you did this alone. Once your pattern is released, the hope is that people do a keyword search on your pattern design. But if you're only relying on people typing in certain words in the search bar menu, the likelihood of getting an influx of traffic coming to your site is small.

Nowadays, bringing in traffic is more than just figuring out what SEO keywords to use. It's about understanding the algorithm, or curating the data and statistics, behind sales sites and social media platforms. As a seller, you want money coming in. Well, so does your online shop platform.

These marketplaces want all small businesses on their platforms to succeed, but more so for the design-sellers who are "the talk of the town." When people share and like your pattern post on social media, it'll increase traffic to your sales platform site in general. "Reputation building" from different sources helps increase traffic. Social media apps and sales sites track how popular your products are. For example, once Etsy knows your pattern is a potential winner, the algorithm will drive the ranking of your pattern to the top of the Etsy search list. Etsy might even use your pattern post as a recommendation for others to consider. When you make money, your platform makes money, too. This is why leveraging multiple platforms and your village of crocheters is so essential.

Search Engine Optimization

ON PAGE SEO	OFF PAGE SEO
✓ Page Title	✓ Social media
✓ Meta description	✓ Ratings and reviews
✓ Image text	✓ Direct link building
✓ Quality Content	✓ Influencer marketing
✓ Headings	✓ Blog posts
✓ Links	✓ Guest posting and commenting

"Keep your face always toward the sunshine, and shadows will fall behind you." Walt Whitman

Choose Your Words Wisely

Take the time to research and write down a list of keywords and phrases that may relate to your pattern to help draw crocheters to your site. The purpose of developing the best use of words to include in your posting is to make it easy for potential customers to find you.

A good way to choose optimal words for your posting is to type in keywords in the search bar menu yourself and just experiment. See what results come up. Are similar patterns to yours popping up? If not, you may have to play around with your wording and fine tune your phrases and descriptive words. It's also important to be creative and unique with your word choices. Keywords as generic as "crochet pattern" may not be very helpful when there are millions of patterns out there. An efficient way to choose the right keywords is to look at your competitor's, and observe *where* they're strategically placing words in their marketing posts.

CHAPTER 9

E IS FOR EMPOWERMENT, EMBRACE, AND ENGAGE

"What would you do if you weren't afraid?" Sheryl Sandberg

1. WHY LOVE OTHERS AND NOT YOURSELF?

Many crocheters join Facebook groups and local crochet clubs to enjoy the company of other crochet hobbyists. Crocheters often praise one another's work, offer constructive but encouraging advice, and provide emotional support for one another. But when looking at our own abilities, we often doubt ourselves. We question our talents, we question our ability to succeed, and we question our self-worth.

So why do we uplift others but don't do the same with ourselves? You often hear crochet can be very therapeutic. Yet, there's a lot of negativity towards oneself, especially when wanting to spread one's talents and teachings to others. It's time to break away from the cycle of negative thoughts.

"Throw me to the wolves and I will return leading the pack." Seneca

---

Don't Let People Suck the Energy Out of You

When people decide to break away from the "norm," others often impose their own opinions on them. If something is different, a fear of the unknown can creep in. As mentioned in Chapter 5, the brain tells us the number one motivational factor in life is satisfying human needs — the need for survival and safety. When one's safety is compromised, people's fears set in. People project their self-doubts and negative thoughts onto you, whether they know and care about you or not.

Most people, frankly, don't have any ill will toward you wanting success. So how does your success directly affect them? It doesn't. Neither friends nor strangers want to see you fail. Naysayers are just projecting their insecurities on you. There's no incentive on their part to have you put money in your own pocket. It's money you're making, not theirs. So, when people put you down, ignore them. Don't let their thoughts become your thoughts.

"Never confuse a single defeat with a final defeat." F. Scott Fitzgerald

---

2. THE SECRET TO TRUE SUCCESS

It Takes a Village

Many wishful thinkers give up too soon or never start a crochet pattern business because they lack a support system. Entrepreneurship is tough, especially for the crocheters out there. Unfortunately, life outside of crochet exists. Crochet entrepreneurs still must manage and juggle life in the real world. There's always someone who still needs to put the kids to bed, cook for the family, and/or go to a 9-to-5 job, and then do it all over again the next day. That someone might be you!

There's only a small sliver of "me" time for running a crochet design business. There's no off switch to your real world, and neither is there an off switch to your design pattern business if you want it to grow. You're trying to juggle this all on your own, and there can be a lot of trials-by-fire in this crochet business.

If you want your business to last, you must take care of yourself first. Don't wear yourself out by doing too much. The "fake it until you make it" mentality in society is pervasive. If you show signs of vulnerability that you're struggling with your side business, then society says that means you're failing. But why does that matter? Don't confuse humility for weakness, and don't put your ego over your business or your wellness.

If you are struggling, why not ask for the help you need? You're better off getting help than struggling alone and shutting down your business. Take the hand that's being offered to you. Maybe all you need are kind words of encouragement, occasional advice here and there, or someone to lend you an ear. Find online interest groups, a crochet mentor, or any support group that can help you out when you're feeling lost and overwhelmed. Entrepreneurship can take a toll on anyone — emotionally, mentally, physically, and even financially. Don't assume you're alone when there are people in the crochet world who can help you.

Outsource Your Weaknesses

When you're first learning, it's best to try every step of the process yourself. But that doesn't mean you have to keep doing everything by yourself. It's important to identify your weaknesses and accept what's working and not working for you. For areas you could be stronger in, look for advice and resources on how to improve. Better yet, outsource your weaknesses.

For example, if you're not a good photographer, take photography classes or have someone you know take photos for you. If you need to improve your social media skills, pay your kids to teach you, or have them do the postings for you. If you want your company to be successful, the best thing to do is delegate and outsource when you can. Either improve so that weaknesses are no longer your weaknesses, or outsource them. Grow yourself or change the business model to grow your business.

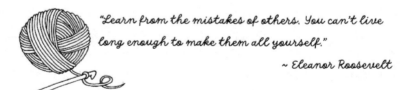

"Learn from the mistakes of others. You can't live long enough to make them all yourself."
~ Eleanor Roosevelt

Imitate Your Admirers

Insanity is when you're doing the same thing over and over again and expecting different results. So before releasing your second pattern, make sure you learn from the mistakes made from your first release. If you want your business to grow exponentially, avoid making repeated mistakes. But more importantly, observe and learn from crochet designers you admire. Ask yourself, why do you admire them? What makes them so special? If you look at their crochet designs, it's not just their talents that make them successful; it's how they present themselves to you and the world. This is the secret to their success.

See how often they post on social media — where they post, what they post, and how they post. What they do, you do. You admire them because you've connected with them. You should learn and adopt this strategy for your design business so others can connect with you as well. For example, does your favorite crochet designer have a Facebook group or a fan page? If so, consider making one for your business. Does your favorite designer have giveaways, post blooper videos, occasionally share free patterns, or collaborate with other designers? If this is what they do, you follow suit. Why start from scratch when you can adopt best practices and lessons learned from others who have already done the guesswork? It's not guesswork anymore but proof! Be a copycat and follow other designers' success patterns (not crochet patterns but business patterns!). If they can succeed, you can too.

"Being good in business is the most fascinating kind of art. Making money is art and working is art and good business is the best art."
Andy Warhol

It's All About Reviews and Customer Loyalty

The toughest part of being a pattern seller is the selling. Accept the fact that most of one's success is figuring out how to market and be efficient at it. Without marketing, there are no sales. Potential buyers don't magically appear on your doorstep. You have to figure out ways for them to come to you.

The first step is for you to post and share in hopes of attracting and directing potential buyers to your pattern site. The second step is to utilize the people around you. Have them post and share on your behalf. The third step is to encourage active buyers to share and review your pattern. Having reviews is one of the most important steps to increasing sales. When others vouch for and endorse your work, there's social proof that your designs and patterns are quite good!

People are more willing to buy your pattern if others praise your work. When you have testimonials, it makes others curious to find out for themselves what all the rave is about. 92% of potential customers look at reviews before purchasing a product, and 88% of purchasing decisions are based on reviews.

The fourth and most crucial step to growing your business is focusing on customer retention. Now that potential buyers have turned into actual buyers, it's your job to keep them. Make sure you make that connection as early as you can. The most valuable customers to have are repeat customers.

Why are repeat customers so crucial to your business? It's all about having their loyalty. Once they have a bond with you and your brand, it's hard to break that bond. Repeat customers make selling easier when they already know who you are. Repeat customers spend 67% more than new customers, as they already know your designs and writing style. Because you've established that connection and trust with repeat customers, it's also much easier to ask them to help you promote your business. Repeat customers bring in 50% more new customers as referrals than one-time customers do. Customer loyalty brings in higher profits. 5% of returning customers bring in 75% of your profits. Repeat customers want to support you, as you would also want to support them and their crochet talents! A successful sales business is built on customer retention.

As you begin to grow your business, take this opportunity to engage with new customers. Send them a thank you coupon code shortly after their purchase to use for next time. As weeks pass, you may wish to check in with them to see how their project is coming along and if they're in need of your assistance. Mention you'd greatly appreciate any feedback they might have so you can become a better designer and pattern writer. Kindly ask them if they're willing to leave a review, preferably with a photo of their finished work, and you'll be glad to send them a discount code. Don't miss out on the opportunity to get acquainted with your customers. You might gain new friendships along the way!

Having a relationship with your customers is truly a beautiful thing. Not only are you bringing joy and the feeling of accomplishment into their lives with your patterns, but they're also making a significant impact in your life. Your return customers want you to succeed in your design pattern business journey. So embrace yourself as a designer.

"It's not the things we get, but the hearts we touch that will measure our success in life." Mac Anderson

---

CONCLUSION:
Today Is The Day

"You're off to great places! Today is your day! Your mountain is waiting. So... get on your way!" Dr. Seuss, Oh the Places You'll Go

Congratulations! You now have everything you need to succeed in your crochet pattern business. This information puts you ahead of other crochet designers starting out. You're ready to start designing, writing, selling, and crushing your competitors. Here are the key takeaways from the 8 essential steps to catapulting your crochet pattern business to success.

S..... is for Shapes and Stitches

✦ Know the craft before you begin this journey.

✦ Understand basic shape patterns.

✦ Have a good concept of increasing and decreasing stitches.

✦ Understand the use of special techniques and stitches.

✦ Check your math.

P..... is for Pop

✦ Put your thoughts down on paper.

✦ Always be on the lookout for inspiration.

✦ Think outside the box.

- ✦ Add a twist to your design to set yourself apart from other designers.
- ✦ Exaggerate your use of colors.
- ✦ Adapt to the new generation of thinking.

R..... is for Report Format

- ✦ Make the best use of what you include in your patterns.
- ✦ Be consistent with your writing and check your math.
- ✦ Offer helpful tips.
- ✦ Ask your customers for help.

I..... is for Inviting

- ✦ First impressions do matter.
- ✦ Post, post, post! And post some more!
- ✦ Connect with emotions.

N..... is for Niche

- ✦ Find your niche and stick with it.
- ✦ Listen to what the consumers want.
- ✦ If at first you don't succeed, try again with improvements
- ✦ Be open to an alternative route of designing and selling.

K..... is for Kinks and Kick-off

- ✦ Seek out pattern testers.
- ✦ Don't be afraid to ask for help.

L..... is for Launch

- ✦ Know your worth and learn to price right.
- ✦ Use a variety of platforms.
- ✦ Know the power of search engine optimization.

E..... is for Empowerment, Embrace, and Engage

- ✦ Do what you can within your capacity.
- ✦ Turn criticism into fuel.

- ✦ Accept your limitations and then outsource them.
- ✦ Imitation is the sincerest form of flattery.
- ✦ Repeat customers!
- ✦ Maximize engagement.

Remember, you've got this! The first step to success is all about starting. So start! The sprinkle of success starts with you today! Just remember to pace yourself on this new endeavor. Be proud of what you're doing, and don't let anyone tell you otherwise. Good luck on this crochet venture, and happy designing!

~~~

If you found this book insightful and helpful, be sure to leave a review so other crocheters can benefit from your unique perspective. Thank you. To your success!

Appendix

Curious To Read More?

From the author

Thank you so much for taking the time to read this book. I hope you found the information helpful as you begin your journey! It has been a pleasure sharing my knowledge with you.

If you're interested to learn more about my upcoming projects or receive early copies of my books (*for free*), please subscribe.

You can sign up at:

https://linktr.ee/CrochetWithConfidence

With much appreciation and respect,

~Elisa

Image Credits

A very special thanks and a big shout-out to the designers who have agreed to showcase their beautiful artistry for this book. Thank you for the encouragement as well. It truly means *a lot*!

Crochet designers mentioned in alphabetical order:

~~~

Airali Design | @airali_gray | www.airalidesign.com | Chapter 2.3, Chapter 3.1, Chapter 3.4, Chapter 5.1

Amiguruku | @amiguruku | www.etsy.com/shop/Amiguruku | Chapter 3.4

Aradiya Toys | @aradiyatoys | www.etsy.com/shop/AradiyaToys | Chapter 3.4

Audrey Lilian Crochet | @audrey__lc | www.etsy.com/shop/AudreyLilianCrochet | Chapter 3.4

Blue Rabbit Toys | @bluerabbittoys | www.etsy.com/shop/BlueRabbitToys | Chapter 3.2, Chapter 5.1

Chai Coffee Crochet | @chaicoffeecrochet | www.chaicoffeecrochet.com | Chapter 5.3

Curious Papaya | @curiouspapaya | www.curiouspapaya.com | Chapter 3.4, Chapter 5.1

Emi Creations By Chloe | @emi_creations | www.emicreations.com.au | Chapter 2.2, Chapter 3.4

Funny Rabbit Toys | www.etsy.com/shop/FunnyRabbitToys | Chapter 2.3, Chapter 2.3 Chapter. 3.4

Crochet Patterns

The crochet designers in this book are delighted to share patterns with the readers! Enjoy and happy crocheting!

 **Audrey Lilian Crochet** | Donut Bunny

 **Curious Papaya** | Gertrude the Grumpy Chick | Chapter 3.4

 **Mikado Cutes** | Bunny

 **Emi Creations by Chloe** | Louie the Bear

 **Julia Ka Patterns** | Squid

 **Storyland Amis** | Lyla the Little Lamb

 **Lucy Magic Pattern** | Gnome

 **Chai Coffee Crochet** | Mika the Monkey

References

Anas, Brittney. (2020, May 26). *Understanding color theory: the color wheel and finding complementary colors.* https://www.invisionapp.com/inside-design/understanding-color-theory-the-color-wheel-and-finding-complementary-colors.

Bailey, Jonathan. (2014, October 8). *Copyrighting in Knitting and Crocheting.* Plagiarism Today. https://www.plagiarismtoday.com/2014/10/08/copyright-in-knitting-and-crocheting.

Baird, Nikki. (2017, January 10). *Last Call For Alcohol At Starbucks.* Forbes. https://www.forbes.com/sites/nikkibaird/2017/01/10/last-call-for-alcohol-at-starbucks/?sh=7741b9502993.

Botta, Attilio. (2020, February 27). *5 reasons why your marketing needs images (and how to use them).* Bynder. https://www.bynder.com/en/blog/the-impact-of-images.

Bruder, Jessica. (2013, September). *Psychological Price of Entrepreneurship.* Inc Magazine. https://www.inc.com/magazine/201309/jessica-bruder/psychological-price-of-entrepreneurship.html.

Can You Draw a Celebrity and Sell It? (n.d.). Art and Prosper. https://artandprosper.com/can-you-draw-a-celebrity-and-sell-it.

Carter, Rebekah. (2021, July 21). *Instagram 101: What's An Instagram Handle And How Do You Choose The Best One?* Kiksta. https://blog.kicksta.co/instagram-handle.

Cheryl. (n.d.). *Crochet Stitch Heights*. Crochet 365 Knit Too. https://www.crochet365knittoo.com/crochet-stitch-heights/.

Childers, Krista. (n.d.). *How Many Crochet Stitches Are There?* All Free Crochet. https://www.allfreecrochet.com/Basics/How-Many-Crochet-Stitches-Are-There.

Decker, Allie. (2018, August 10). *The Ultimate Guide to Emotional Marketing*. https://blog.hubspot.com/marketing/emotion-marketing.

Decker, Ivy. (2018, May 9). *Knitting and Crochet Today: Statistics, Trends, and More*. The Maker Files. https://blog.anthonythomas.com/knitting-and-crochet-today-statistics-trends-and-more.

Differences Between Plagiarism and Similarity. (2022, February 19). Writer's King Ltd. https://writersking.com/plagiarism-and-similarity.

Divisible. (n.d.) Splash Learn. https://www.splashlearn.com/math-vocabulary/division/divisible.

Does, Dora. (n.d.). *Crochet Explained: What are stitch multiples?* https://doradoes.co.uk/2020/02/29/crochet-explained-what-is-a-stitch-multiple.

Etsy Vs. Ravelry Vs. Lovecrafts – How to Sell Knitting and Crochet Patterns Online, Risk Free. (2020, March 25). The Snugglery. https://thesnugglery.net/etsy-vs-ravelry-vs-lovecrafts-how-to-sell-knitting-and-crochet-patterns-online-risk-free.

Everything You Need to Know About Pattern Testing. (n.d.). Woods and Wool. https://www.woodsandwool.com/everything-need-know-pattern-testing.

Ferguson, Corinnia. (n.d.). *Back Loop, Front Loop, or Both?* Creative Crochet Corner. https://www.creativecrochet-corner.com/article/back-loop-front-loop-or-both.

Finding Your Design Niche. (2016, August 10). Ambassador Crochet. https://ambassadorcrochet.com/2016/08/10/how-to-find-your-designing-niche.

Girard, Jeremy. (2022, June 9). Visual Color Symbolism Chart by Culture. https://www.thoughtco.com/visual-color-symbolism-chart-by-culture-4062177.

Hinkley, William, Heffernan, N., and Bouygues, H.L. (2020, March). *The Benefits of Using Pencil and Paper in Math.* Reboot. https://reboot-foundation.org/pencil-and-paper-in-math.

How similar is too similar? (2018, February 18). https://www.plagiarism.org/blog/2018/02/27/how-similar-is-too-similar.

How to Crochet a Ball in Any Size - Amigurumi Design Basics. (2021, September 27). Ollie and Holly. https://www.ollieholly.com/blog/2021/09/27/how-to-crochet-a-ball-in-any-size-amigurumi-design-basics.

How to Crochet Cones in Spiral Rounds. (n.d.). Supergurumi. https://www.supergurumi.com/how-to-crochet-cones-in-spiral-rounds.

How To Photograph your Crochet and Make Yourself Stand Out on Instagram. (n.d.). Sigoni Macaroni. https://www.sigonimacaroni.com/how-to-photograph-crochet-and-stand-out-on-instagram.

How to Photograph Your Crochet Projects. (2020, July 2). Bella Coco Crochet. https://blog.bellacococrochet.com/how-to-photograph-your-crochet-projects.

How to Photograph Your Crochet. (2015, January 19). Repeat Crafter Me. https://www.repeatcrafterme.com/2015/01/how-to-photograph-your-crochet.html.

Is the Wizard of Oz in the Public Domain? (2020, October 27). New Media Rights. https://www.newmediarights.org/business_models/artist/wizard_oz_public_domain.

Kati. (2019, August 27). *Basic Amigurumi Shapes: The Shape Is In The Math*. Hooked By Katie. https://www.hookedbykati. com/basic-amigurumi-shapes-the-shape-is-in-the-math.

Kristina. (n.d.). *How to Design Your Own Amigurumi Pattern*. Tiny Curl. https://www.tinycurl.co/how-to-design-amiguru-mi-crochet-pattern/#step9

Landwer-Johan, Kevin. (n.d.). *How to Use Photography Props for Great Portraits*. Expert Photography. https://expertpho-tography.com/portrait-photography-props.

Lee, Benjamin. (2020). *72% Of Entrepreneurs Suffer From Mental Health Issues. Here's Why—And What To Do About It*. Minute. https://minutes.co/72-of-entrepreneurs-suffer-from-mental-health-issues-heres-why-and-what-to-do-about-it.

Liana. (2020, July). *What Crochet Stitch Works up the Fastest? (We Time 16 Stitches)*. The School of Crochet. https:// schoolofcrochet.com/what-crochet-stitch-works-up-the-fastest-we-time-16-stitches.

Little, Ashley. (n.d.). *British vs. American Crochet Terms: What's the Difference?* Craftsy. https://www.craftsy.com/post/brit-ish-vs-american-crochet-terms.

Little, Ashley. (n.d.). *Here's How to Back Loop Crochet Belongs in Your Next Project*. Craftsy. https://www.craftsy.com/post/back-loop-crochet.

Littlejohn, Alysha. (n.d.). *How to Copyright a Crochet Pattern*. Littlejohn's Yarn. https://littlejohnsyarn.com/are-cro-chet-stitches-copyrighted.

Maccarone, Dan. (2013, January). *The Beauty Bias: Good-looking women may actually have a harder time landing some jobs*. Psychology Today. https://www.psychologytoday.com/gb/articles/200301/the-beauty-bias.

Makridakis, Spyros. (2015, June 30). *The cost and benefits of positive illusions*. Frontiers in Psychology. https://www.ncbi.nlm.nih.gov/pmc/articles/PMC4485033.

Marketing Theories - Maslow's Hierarchy of Needs. (n.d.). Professional Academy. https://www.professionalacademy.com/blogs/marketing-theories-maslows-hierarchy-of-needs.

Mathematics. (n.d.). Wikipedia. https://en.wikipedia.org/wiki/Mathematics

My Foolproof Guide to Crocheting Amigurumi for Beginners in 2022. (2022, February 10). Little World of Whimsy. https://littleworldofwhimsy.com/my-foolproof-guide-to-crocheting-amigurumi-for-beginners.

Nethercott, Rustin. (2022, July 6). *5 Reasons Why Repeat Customers Are Better Than New Customers.* Constant Contact. https://www.constantcontact.com/blog/repeat-customers.

Pattern Testing Questions & Answers. (2020, November 10). Edie Eckman. https://www.edieeckman.com/2020/11/10/pattern-testing-questions-and-answers.

Pengetti, Martin. (2021, January 28). *Crochet artist turns viral Bernie Sanders image into a doll that sells for $20,000.* The Guardian. https://www.theguardian.com/us-news/2021/jan/27/bernie-sanders-meme-crochet-doll.

Russell, Shawndra. (n.d.). *5 smart ways to use Canva for social media.* Canva. https://www.canva.com/learn/5-smart-ways-to-use-canva-for-social-media.

Sliwa, Jim. (2016). *Self-Esteem Gender Gap More Pronounced in Western Countries.* American Psychology Association. https://www.apa.org/news/press/releases/2016/01/self-esteem-gender.

Stemler, Sam. (2021, February 1). *30 Impactful Statistics About Using Testimonials In Marketing.* Boast. https://boast.io/20-statistics-about-using-testimonials-in-marketing.

Tardi, Karla. (2022, July 2). *The 80-20 Rule (aka Pareto Principle): What It Is, How It Works.* Investopedia. https://www.investopedia.com/terms/1/80-20-rule.asp.

Teaching Dividend, Divisor, and Quotient in Division. (2021, March 3). https://www.hmhco.com/blog/teaching-dividend-divisor-and-quotient-in-division.

The convenience factor: 6 ways to capitalize on this shopper preference. (2020, March 20). https://www.sfgnetwork.com/blog/customer-care/the-convenience-factor-6-ways-to-capitalize-on-this-shopper-preference.

U.S. Copyright Office. https://www.copyright.gov.

What Is SEO & Why Is It Important. (2021, October 18). Digital Marketing Institute. https://digitalmarketinginstitute.com/blog/what-is-seo-and-why-is-it-important

Where to Sell Knitting Patterns Online: A Summary of Online Platforms for Selling Knitting Patterns (2021, July 20). Snickerdoodle Knits. https://www.snickerdoodleknits.com/post/where-to-sell-knitting-patterns-online-a-summary-of-online-platforms-for-selling-knitting-patterns.

Why Should Students Show Their Work. (2017, November 2). A Grade Ahead. https://blog.agradeahead.com/post/students-show-work.

5 Tips for Photographing Crochet. (2019, September 16). Pattern Paradise. https://pattern-paradise.com/2019/09/06/5-tips-for-photographing-crochet.

60 Social Proof Statistics You Must Read: 2022 Data Analysis & Market Share. (n.d.). Finances Online. https://financesonline.com/social-proof-statistics.

Bonus Sample

~ An excerpt from ~

The Student Becomes the Amigurumi Crochet Master

A Beginner's Success Guide to Designing Crochet Patterns: The 9-Day Amigurumi Challenge

It's important to design works that are evergreen. What does it mean by evergreen besides a tree with pine needles? Evergreen is when your work never grows old or goes out of style. When's the busiest time of the year when you crochet? When do most people make the most purchases on anything during the year? Crocheters are often the busiest right before the holiday season because of the uptick in interest and demand for giving and sharing for the holidays. Focus your designs with the holiday season in mind. You'll happily get recurring orders throughout the year and every year!

Printed in Great Britain
by Amazon

32673937R00089